The Cuban Missile Crisis: Unraveling Khruschev's Rule

Copyright Page

TITLE: The Cuban Missile Crisis: Unraveling Khruschev's Rule

1ST Edition

Copyright @ 2023

ISBN: 9798223583646

Table of Contents

Title Page 1

The Cuban Missile Crisis: Unraveling Khrushchev's Rule...................7

Chapter 1: The Role of the Cuban Missile Crisis in the Fall of Nikita Khrushchev 8

Chapter 2: Khrushchev's Agricultural Policies and Their Impact on His Downfall 16

Chapter 3: Khrushchev's Relationship with the Soviet Military and Its Role in His Removal from Power 23

Chapter 4: The Role of Economic Reforms in Khrushchev's Downfall 30

Chapter 5: Khrushchev's De-Stalinization Campaign and Its Impact on His Political Standing 38

Chapter 6: Khrushchev's Handling of the Soviet Space Program and Its Influence on His Fall from Power 45

Chapter 7: Khrushchev's Foreign Policy Decisions and Their Role in His Downfall 52

Chapter 4: The Impact of Foreign Policy on Khrushchev's Loss of Power 58

Chapter 8: Khrushchev's Relationship with the Eastern Bloc Countries and Its Impact on His Removal from Power 61

Chapter 9: Khrushchev's Attempt to Reform the Soviet Political System and Its Role in His Downfall................................... 68

Chapter 10: Khrushchev's Personality and Leadership Style and How They Contributed to His Fall from Power 77

The Cuban Missile Crisis: Unraveling Khrushchev's Rule

By Roberto Miguel Rodriguez

Chapter 1: The Role of the Cuban Missile Crisis in the Fall of Nikita Khrushchev

The Origins and Buildup of the Cuban Missile Crisis

The Cuban Missile Crisis was a pivotal moment in history, and understanding its origins and buildup is essential to unraveling the rule of Nikita Khrushchev. This subchapter explores the events leading up to the crisis and sheds light on its significance in Khrushchev's downfall.

Khrushchev's agricultural policies played a significant role in his fall from power. His attempts to modernize and increase agricultural production through the Virgin Lands Campaign and the introduction of maize cultivation were met with resistance and failure. These policies resulted in food shortages and discontent among the Soviet population, weakening Khrushchev's political standing.

Another factor in Khrushchev's removal from power was his relationship with the Soviet military. Despite being a former military officer himself, Khrushchev faced opposition from the military establishment due to his attempts to reduce its influence and prioritize economic development over military spending. The Cuban Missile Crisis further strained this relationship as the military felt undermined by Khrushchev's handling of the crisis.

Economic reforms also played a crucial role in Khrushchev's downfall. His attempts to decentralize economic planning through the introduction of regional economic councils and his focus on consumer goods production were met with resistance and led to economic inefficiencies. These failures further eroded Khrushchev's political standing and contributed to his removal from power.

Khrushchev's de-Stalinization campaign, aimed at criticizing and distancing the Soviet Union from the excesses of Stalin's rule, had a significant impact on his political standing. While this campaign initially gained him support, it also created divisions within the party and the Soviet bureaucracy, ultimately contributing to his downfall.

Khrushchev's foreign policy decisions, including his handling of the Cuban Missile Crisis, also played a role in his removal from power. The crisis, which brought the world to the brink of nuclear war, highlighted Khrushchev's inability to effectively navigate international relations and manage conflicts. This failure further weakened his political position.

Khrushchev's relationships with Eastern Bloc countries, particularly his attempts to assert Soviet dominance and control, also contributed to his removal from power. His interference in the internal affairs of these countries created tensions and led to a loss of support among Eastern Bloc leaders.

Furthermore, Khrushchev's attempt to reform the Soviet political system by introducing collective leadership and reducing the power of the party elite faced resistance and backlash. These reforms were seen as threatening to the established order and ultimately contributed to his downfall.

Lastly, Khrushchev's personality and leadership style played a significant role in his fall from power. His erratic behavior, impulsive decision-making, and tendency to make grandiose speeches without proper planning or consultation alienated many within the party and the Soviet bureaucracy.

In conclusion, the origins and buildup of the Cuban Missile Crisis shed light on the multiple factors that contributed to Nikita Khrushchev's downfall. His agricultural policies, strained relationship with the military, economic failures, de-Stalinization campaign, foreign policy decisions, relationships with Eastern Bloc countries, attempts to reform the political system, and his leadership style all played a role in his removal from power. Understanding these complexities is essential for diplomats, historians, and politicians seeking to comprehend the unraveling of Khrushchev's rule.

Khrushchev's Decision to Deploy Missiles in Cuba

The Cuban Missile Crisis is often regarded as a pivotal event in the downfall of Nikita Khrushchev's rule. This subchapter delves into the intricate details of Khrushchev's decision to deploy missiles in Cuba, shedding light on its significance and consequences.

Khrushchev's agricultural policies played a crucial role in his downfall, leaving the Soviet Union struggling to feed its population. The decision to deploy missiles in Cuba can be seen as an attempt to divert attention from these failures. By asserting Soviet power in the Western Hemisphere, Khrushchev aimed to regain prestige and divert domestic discontent.

Furthermore, Khrushchev's relationship with the Soviet military proved to be a double-edged sword. While he sought to modernize and strengthen the armed forces, this move created tensions and rivalries within the military hierarchy. These tensions ultimately played a part in his removal from power.

Economic reforms also played a significant role in Khrushchev's downfall. His attempts to decentralize economic decision-making and introduce market mechanisms faced resistance from conservative elements in the party. These economic reforms, coupled with agricultural failures, weakened Khrushchev's political standing and provided ammunition for his opponents.

Khrushchev's de-Stalinization campaign, aimed at dismantling the cult of personality surrounding Joseph Stalin, also contributed to his political standing. While initially popular, this campaign alienated conservative elements within the party who saw it as a threat to their power. This, in turn, facilitated the opposition's efforts to remove Khrushchev from power.

In the realm of foreign policy, Khrushchev's decisions had far-reaching implications. The deployment of missiles in Cuba was an audacious move, but it came with great risks. The crisis strained Soviet relations with the United States and its allies, further isolating Khrushchev in the international arena.

Khrushchev's relationship with the Eastern Bloc countries also played a role in his downfall. His attempts to assert Soviet dominance and control over these nations bred resentment and resistance. This, combined with the economic and political challenges faced by these countries, resulted in a loss of support for Khrushchev within the Eastern Bloc.

Khrushchev's personality and leadership style also contributed to his fall from power. His impulsive and often erratic behavior alienated party elites and undermined his authority. His handling of the Soviet space program, while initially successful, eventually became a liability as costly failures mounted.

In conclusion, Khrushchev's decision to deploy missiles in Cuba was a pivotal event in his downfall. This subchapter explores the multifaceted factors that contributed to this decision and its consequences. From agricultural policies to economic reforms, from foreign policy decisions to his personality and leadership style, each aspect sheds light on the complex dynamics that ultimately led to Khrushchev's removal from power.

The United States' Response and the Escalation of Tensions

The Cuban Missile Crisis was a pivotal moment in history that had far-reaching consequences, not only for the United States and Soviet

Union but also for the world as a whole. This subchapter explores the United States' response to the crisis and how it contributed to the escalation of tensions between the two superpowers.

When the United States first discovered the presence of Soviet missiles in Cuba, President John F. Kennedy faced a difficult decision. The existence of these missiles posed a direct threat to American national security, and a swift response was needed to prevent any potential nuclear conflict. Kennedy, in consultation with his advisors, decided on a strategy of both military readiness and diplomacy.

The United States immediately implemented a naval blockade, known as a "quarantine," around Cuba to prevent further Soviet shipments of military equipment. This move was a direct challenge to Soviet Premier Nikita Khrushchev's authority and indicated the seriousness of the situation. The blockade was a calculated response, aimed at avoiding an all-out war while still pressuring the Soviet Union to remove the missiles.

Simultaneously, Kennedy engaged in secret negotiations with Khrushchev, utilizing backchannel diplomacy to defuse the crisis. These negotiations were tense and often uncertain, with both sides trying to assert their interests and avoid a catastrophic outcome. Ultimately, a deal was struck: the United States agreed to remove its Jupiter missiles from Turkey, and the Soviet Union agreed to dismantle its missile bases in Cuba.

However, while the crisis was averted, it had lasting implications for the Cold War and Khrushchev's rule. The United States' response and the escalation of tensions during the crisis highlighted Khrushchev's inability to effectively manage the situation. His agricultural policies, which included the Virgin Lands Campaign and the focus on corn cultivation, had already caused widespread food shortages and economic instability in the Soviet Union. The Cuban Missile Crisis further exposed Khrushchev's weaknesses as a leader and eroded his support within the Soviet military.

Furthermore, Khrushchev's foreign policy decisions, such as the failed attempt to install missiles in Cuba, damaged his reputation both domestically and internationally. His handling of the Soviet space program, while initially seen as a symbol of Soviet technological prowess, ultimately failed to achieve its goals and further undermined his authority.

In conclusion, the United States' response to the Cuban Missile Crisis and the subsequent escalation of tensions played a significant role in the fall of Nikita Khrushchev. The crisis exposed his weaknesses as a leader, including his agricultural policies, relationship with the Soviet military, and foreign policy decisions. Ultimately, these factors contributed to his removal from power and reshaped the geopolitical landscape of the Cold War era.

The Role of the Cuban Missile Crisis in Khrushchev's Loss of Power

Title: The Role of the Cuban Missile Crisis in Khrushchev's Loss of Power

Introduction:

In the annals of history, few events have had such a profound impact on a leader's downfall as the Cuban Missile Crisis had on Nikita Khrushchev's political career. This subchapter delves into the intricate web of factors that culminated in Khrushchev's removal from power, with a particular focus on the role played by the Cuban Missile Crisis. Examining the crisis within the context of Khrushchev's agricultural policies, relationship with the Soviet military, economic reforms, de-Stalinization campaign, foreign policy decisions, and attempts to reform the Soviet political system, we gain a comprehensive understanding of how this pivotal event contributed to his eventual fall from power.

The Cuban Missile Crisis: A Turning Point:

The Cuban Missile Crisis, which unfolded in October 1962, marked a significant turning point in Khrushchev's rule. By secretly deploying nuclear missiles in Cuba, Khrushchev aimed to counterbalance the United States' nuclear presence in Turkey and protect Cuba from potential American aggression. However, this bold move proved disastrous for Khrushchev's political standing.

Impact on Agricultural Policies:

Khrushchev's ambitious agricultural policies, such as the Virgin Lands Campaign, aimed at boosting agricultural productivity and alleviating food shortages. However, the diversion of resources to fund the missile deployment led to a decline in agricultural output, exacerbating food scarcity and eroding public support for Khrushchev.

Role of the Soviet Military:

Khrushchev's strained relationship with the Soviet military further contributed to his downfall. The military's dissatisfaction with his de-Stalinization campaign, coupled with the perceived humiliation resulting from the resolution of the Cuban Missile Crisis, eroded Khrushchev's authority and emboldened his opponents.

Economic Reforms and De-Stalinization:

Khrushchev's economic reforms, marked by the shift from heavy industry to consumer goods production, faced significant resistance. The Cuban Missile Crisis strained the Soviet economy, exposing the flaws in Khrushchev's policies and weakening his position, as economic stability was crucial in maintaining political support.

Foreign Policy Decisions and Eastern Bloc Relations:

Khrushchev's foreign policy decisions, including the Berlin Crisis and the Cuban Missile Crisis, strained relations with the United States and the Eastern Bloc countries. The Cuban Missile Crisis brought the world to the brink of nuclear war, damaging Khrushchev's international reputation and isolating him further within the Eastern Bloc.

Khrushchev's Leadership Style and Personality:

Khrushchev's brash and impulsive leadership style, coupled with his volatile personality, alienated key supporters and fueled opposition within the Soviet leadership. The Cuban Missile Crisis, with its high-stakes brinkmanship, exposed these weaknesses and eroded confidence in his ability to lead effectively.

Conclusion:

The Cuban Missile Crisis served as a catalyst for Khrushchev's removal from power, exacerbating existing tensions and weaknesses within his regime. By analyzing the crisis in conjunction with Khrushchev's agricultural policies, relationship with the military, economic reforms, de-Stalinization campaign, foreign policy decisions, attempts at political reform, and personality traits, we gain valuable insights into the multifaceted factors that led to his downfall. The lessons learned from this pivotal event continue to shape diplomatic and political discourse, reminding us of the delicate nature of leadership and the far-reaching consequences of critical decision-making.

Chapter 2: Khrushchev's Agricultural Policies and Their Impact on His Downfall

The Virgin Lands Campaign and its Objectives

The Virgin Lands Campaign, launched by Soviet leader Nikita Khrushchev in 1953, was a massive agricultural initiative aimed at increasing grain production in the Soviet Union. This subchapter will delve into the objectives of the campaign and its significance in understanding the fall of Khrushchev's rule.

One of the primary objectives of the Virgin Lands Campaign was to boost agricultural output to address the Soviet Union's growing food demands. Khrushchev envisioned transforming the vast uncultivated lands of Kazakhstan, Siberia, and other regions into fertile agricultural areas. By encouraging peasants and volunteers to settle in these "virgin lands" and cultivate them, Khrushchev hoped to increase grain production and make the Soviet Union self-sufficient in food.

Another objective of the campaign was to showcase the superiority of the Soviet socialist system over the capitalist West. Khrushchev believed that a successful agricultural initiative would not only prove the efficiency of Soviet planning but also undermine the capitalist world's claims of economic superiority. By demonstrating the potential for rapid agricultural growth, Khrushchev aimed to strengthen the Soviet Union's global standing and inspire other socialist countries to follow suit.

However, the Virgin Lands Campaign did not fully achieve its objectives and had unintended consequences that contributed to Khrushchev's downfall. While the campaign initially resulted in a surge in grain production, the long-term sustainability of the agricultural practices employed was questionable. The rush to cultivate the virgin lands led to ecological damage, soil erosion, and inadequate infrastructure, hampering productivity in subsequent years.

Furthermore, the campaign diverted resources and attention away from other sectors, including industry, defense, and consumer goods production. This had a negative impact on the Soviet economy, leading to shortages and discontent among the population. Khrushchev's agricultural policies were seen as a misallocation of resources, exacerbating existing economic issues and undermining his credibility as a leader.

The Virgin Lands Campaign also strained Khrushchev's relationship with the Soviet military. The diversion of resources to the agricultural sector meant reduced funding for the military, which caused dissatisfaction among the military leadership. This discontent, combined with other factors such as Khrushchev's handling of the Cuban Missile Crisis and his foreign policy decisions, contributed to his removal from power in 1964.

In conclusion, the Virgin Lands Campaign was a significant initiative in Khrushchev's agricultural policies. While it aimed to increase grain production and showcase the superiority of the Soviet system, the campaign had unintended consequences that contributed to Khrushchev's downfall. The misallocation of resources, strain on the economy, and strained relationship with the military all played a role in undermining Khrushchev's political standing and ultimately led to his removal from power. Understanding the objectives and consequences of the Virgin Lands Campaign provides valuable insight into the complexities of Khrushchev's rule and the factors that contributed to his fall from power.

Challenges and Failures of Khrushchev's Agricultural Reforms

Khrushchev's agricultural policies played a significant role in his downfall as the leader of the Soviet Union. His ambitious attempts to modernize and improve the agricultural sector faced numerous challenges and ultimately resulted in failures that undermined his political standing. This subchapter explores the key obstacles and shortcomings of Khrushchev's agricultural reforms.

One of the major challenges Khrushchev faced was the resistance from the Soviet bureaucracy and the entrenched interests of the collective farm system. The collectivization process initiated by Stalin had created a rigid and inefficient system that was resistant to change. Khrushchev's attempts to introduce larger-scale farming and mechanization faced opposition from the collective farm managers who feared losing their power and influence. This resistance hindered the implementation of Khrushchev's agricultural reforms and prevented the necessary changes from taking root.

Moreover, Khrushchev's policies were hindered by a lack of expertise and resources necessary for modernizing agriculture. The Soviet Union lagged behind the West in terms of technological advancements and scientific knowledge in agriculture. The lack of access to modern machinery, fertilizers, and advanced farming techniques further hampered the effectiveness of Khrushchev's reforms. Additionally, the vastness of the Soviet Union presented logistical challenges in distributing resources and coordinating efforts.

Another significant failure of Khrushchev's agricultural reforms was the inability to increase food production to meet the growing demands of the population. Despite promising higher yields and increased efficiency, the reforms fell short of expectations. Agricultural production remained stagnant, and shortages persisted. This failure undermined Khrushchev's credibility and eroded public support for his leadership.

Furthermore, Khrushchev's agricultural policies had negative environmental consequences. The focus on maximizing output led to overuse of fertilizers and pesticides, causing soil degradation and pollution. These environmental concerns, coupled with the failure to meet production targets, further undermined Khrushchev's legitimacy as a leader capable of addressing the pressing challenges facing the Soviet Union.

In conclusion, Khrushchev's agricultural reforms faced significant challenges and resulted in failures that contributed to his downfall. The resistance from the collective farm system, the lack of expertise and resources, the failure to increase food production, and the negative environmental impact all played a role in undermining Khrushchev's political standing. The shortcomings of his agricultural policies exposed his inability to effectively address the economic needs of the country, ultimately contributing to his removal from power.

The Impact of Agricultural Shortages on Khrushchev's Political Standing

One of the key factors that led to the fall of Nikita Khrushchev's rule was the agricultural shortages that plagued the Soviet Union during his time in power. These shortages had a significant impact on Khrushchev's political standing, contributing to the dissatisfaction among the Soviet people and the loss of support from key factions within the Soviet government.

Khrushchev's agricultural policies were at the heart of his economic reforms. He aimed to increase agricultural production through the implementation of collective farms and the use of chemical fertilizers. However, these policies proved to be ineffective and led to widespread inefficiencies in the agricultural sector. The collective farms lacked proper incentives for the farmers, resulting in low productivity levels.

Additionally, the overuse of chemical fertilizers led to soil degradation, further exacerbating the problem.

The consequences of these agricultural failures were far-reaching. The Soviet Union faced severe food shortages, with staple crops such as grain and potatoes in short supply. This led to rationing and long queues for basic food items, causing public discontent and a loss of faith in Khrushchev's ability to govern effectively.

Furthermore, Khrushchev's agricultural failures had a significant impact on his relationship with the Soviet military. The military, a crucial pillar of support for any Soviet leader, relied on a stable food supply to maintain morale and readiness. The shortages strained the military's resources and weakened their confidence in Khrushchev's leadership.

The agricultural shortages also highlighted the broader economic problems facing the Soviet Union under Khrushchev's rule. The failure of his economic reforms to deliver the promised results undermined his credibility and contributed to growing opposition within the Soviet government. Factions within the Communist Party, particularly those aligned with more conservative, Stalinist ideals, capitalized on these failures to challenge Khrushchev's authority.

In conclusion, the agricultural shortages that occurred under Khrushchev's rule had a profound impact on his political standing. They not only caused widespread dissatisfaction among the Soviet people but also eroded support from key factions within the government and the military. These shortages exposed the failures of Khrushchev's agricultural policies and economic reforms, ultimately contributing to his downfall.

Opposition to Khrushchev's Agricultural Policies and Its Role in His Removal

Throughout his rule, Nikita Khrushchev faced numerous challenges that ultimately led to his removal from power. One significant factor that contributed to his downfall was the strong opposition he faced regarding his agricultural policies. This subchapter will delve into the reasons behind the opposition and how it played a pivotal role in Khrushchev's removal from office.

Khrushchev's agricultural policies aimed to increase food production and improve the quality of life for Soviet citizens. However, the methods he employed, such as the Virgin Lands Campaign and the collectivization of agriculture, faced significant opposition from various sections of society.

Firstly, farmers and rural communities were vehemently opposed to Khrushchev's policies. The collectivization efforts disrupted traditional farming practices and forced individual farmers to give up their land and livestock. This led to a decline in productivity and a decrease in agricultural output, resulting in food shortages and discontent among the population.

Secondly, Khrushchev's policies faced resistance from members within the Soviet bureaucracy. Many high-ranking officials believed that the agricultural reforms were hasty and ill-planned. They argued that Khrushchev's focus on quantity over quality led to a decline in agricultural efficiency. The opposition within the bureaucracy grew stronger as agricultural failures persisted, eroding Khrushchev's support base.

Furthermore, Khrushchev's agricultural policies also faced opposition from the Soviet military. The military leaders were concerned that the focus on agriculture was diverting resources away from defense and jeopardizing national security. This opposition from the military, combined with the discontent within the bureaucracy and rural communities, dealt a severe blow to Khrushchev's authority.

The opposition to Khrushchev's agricultural policies played a crucial role in his removal from power. It weakened his position within the Soviet leadership, eroded his support base, and created divisions within the Party. Eventually, Khrushchev's adversaries seized the opportunity to remove him from office, using his failures in agriculture as a pretext.

In conclusion, the strong opposition to Khrushchev's agricultural policies significantly contributed to his downfall. Farmers, bureaucrats, and the military were all critical of his methods and blamed him for the decline in agricultural productivity. This opposition weakened Khrushchev's position and ultimately provided his adversaries with the opportunity to remove him from power. Understanding the role of agricultural policies in Khrushchev's removal is crucial to comprehending the complex dynamics that shaped his rule and the events surrounding his downfall.

Chapter 3: Khrushchev's Relationship with the Soviet Military and Its Role in His Removal from Power

Khrushchev's Efforts to Consolidate Power within the Military

Title: Khrushchev's Efforts to Consolidate Power within the Military

Introduction:

In the tumultuous era of the Cold War, Nikita Khrushchev's role as the leader of the Soviet Union was marked by a series of significant events. One of the key aspects that shaped his rule was his relentless pursuit to consolidate power within the military. This subchapter delves into Khrushchev's efforts to strengthen his control over the armed forces, shedding light on the factors that contributed to his downfall. Targeting diplomats, historians, and politicians, this section aims to provide a comprehensive understanding of the intricate relationship between Khrushchev and the Soviet military.

Body:

Khrushchev's rise to power was significantly influenced by his successful handling of the Cuban Missile Crisis. However, this event also sowed the seeds of his downfall, as it strained his relationship with the military establishment. Despite his achievements, Khrushchev's agricultural policies and their subsequent failures played a crucial role in undermining his authority within the military. The scarcity of resources caused by his ill-conceived agricultural reforms led to discontentment among the armed forces.

Furthermore, Khrushchev's attempts at de-Stalinization, although popular among the masses, were met with resistance from the military.

The Soviet military had long benefited from Stalin's authoritarian rule and the cult of personality surrounding him. Khrushchev's denunciation of Stalin and his policies, therefore, created a rift between him and the military elite, eroding his support base.

The economic reforms introduced by Khrushchev also contributed to his downfall. His focus on the production of consumer goods and housing, while neglecting military expenditures, eroded the military's confidence in his leadership. This imbalance in resource allocation strained the relationship between Khrushchev and the military, further weakening his grip on power.

Moreover, Khrushchev's foreign policy decisions, such as the mishandling of the Soviet space program and his volatile relationship with Eastern Bloc countries, exacerbated his already fragile position. The military, with its deep-rooted influence, viewed these actions as detrimental to Soviet interests, eroding their faith in Khrushchev's leadership.

Finally, Khrushchev's attempt to reform the Soviet political system, including reducing the power of the Communist Party, threatened the military's traditional role in the governance structure. This move, combined with Khrushchev's impulsive personality and autocratic leadership style, alienated key military figures, ultimately leading to his removal from power.

Conclusion:

Khrushchev's efforts to consolidate power within the military played a pivotal role in his downfall. The combination of failed agricultural policies, strained relationships with the military establishment, economic imbalances, foreign policy missteps, and attempts to reform the Soviet political system ultimately eroded his support base. Understanding these dynamics is crucial for historians, diplomats, and politicians seeking insights into the complex factors that led to Khrushchev's fall from power.

The Cuban Missile Crisis and the Soviet Military's Influence

The Cuban Missile Crisis is often regarded as a critical event in the fall of Nikita Khrushchev's rule. This subchapter delves into the role played by the Soviet military during this tense period, shedding light on its impact on Khrushchev's downfall.

Khrushchev's agricultural policies were one of the main causes of his political downfall. However, the Cuban Missile Crisis amplified the existing discontent within the Soviet military regarding these policies. The military, which had historically enjoyed a significant influence over Soviet politics, saw Khrushchev's agricultural failures as a threat to national security. The crisis further revealed Khrushchev's weaknesses, as his inability to adequately address the military's concerns eroded his support within the ranks.

Khrushchev's relationship with the Soviet military was complex, with both cooperation and tension prevailing. While he sought to modernize and streamline the military, his aggressive foreign policy decisions and the mishandling of the Cuban Missile Crisis strained this relationship. The military felt marginalized and excluded from decision-making processes, leading to a loss of confidence in Khrushchev's leadership.

Economic reforms also played a significant role in Khrushchev's downfall. His attempts to shift resources from heavy industry to agriculture and consumer goods production were met with resistance from the military-industrial complex. As the military-industrial complex held substantial power within the Soviet Union, they actively opposed Khrushchev's economic policies, further weakening his position.

Khrushchev's de-Stalinization campaign, aimed at distancing the Soviet Union from the excesses of Stalin's regime, also impacted his political standing. The military, which held a deep respect for Stalin, viewed this campaign as a betrayal of their values. This alienation from the military, coupled with the growing discontent among Eastern Bloc countries, contributed to Khrushchev's removal from power.

Khrushchev's handling of the Soviet space program also played a role in his fall from power. Despite early successes, the failures and setbacks in the space race damaged Khrushchev's reputation and weakened his authority. The military, which had invested heavily in the space program, saw these failures as a reflection of Khrushchev's poor leadership and lost faith in his ability to guide the country.

In conclusion, the Cuban Missile Crisis amplified the existing tensions between Khrushchev and the Soviet military, ultimately contributing to his downfall. The military's dissatisfaction with his agricultural policies, economic reforms, foreign policy decisions, and handling of the space program all played a significant role in eroding Khrushchev's support and ultimately leading to his removal from power.

Opposition from Military Leaders and its Impact on Khrushchev's Rule

Throughout his rule as the Soviet Primer, Nikita Khrushchev faced significant opposition from military leaders within the Soviet Union. This opposition played a crucial role in the unraveling of Khrushchev's rule and ultimately contributed to his downfall. In this subchapter, we will explore the reasons behind this opposition and its broader impact on the Cuban Missile Crisis, as well as the eventual fall of Khrushchev.

One of the key reasons for the opposition from military leaders was Khrushchev's policy of de-Stalinization. Khrushchev's denunciation of Stalin's repressive regime and his efforts to distance the Soviet Union from Stalin's cult of personality were met with strong resistance from military officials who had risen to power during the Stalin era. Many military leaders saw Khrushchev's actions as a direct threat to their own positions and privileges, leading to a deep-seated resentment and opposition against his rule.

Furthermore, Khrushchev's attempts at reducing military spending and reallocating resources to civilian sectors were met with resistance from military leaders. These leaders believed that a strong military was crucial for the Soviet Union's global standing and were reluctant to support Khrushchev's policies, which they perceived as weakening their own power and influence.

The impact of this opposition on the Cuban Missile Crisis cannot be overstated. Khrushchev's decision to deploy nuclear missiles to Cuba was met with skepticism and resistance from several military leaders who believed it would escalate tensions with the United States. This opposition led to a lack of unity within the Soviet leadership, with some military officials openly challenging Khrushchev's authority and advocating for a more aggressive stance.

The divided leadership weakened Khrushchev's position during the Cuban Missile Crisis and limited his ability to negotiate with the United States. Ultimately, it was the Soviet military leaders' opposition and their insistence on a more confrontational approach that forced Khrushchev to back down and remove the missiles from Cuba, a move that damaged his credibility both domestically and internationally.

The opposition from military leaders also played a significant role in the fall of Khrushchev. The failure of the Cuban Missile Crisis and the subsequent loss of prestige further eroded Khrushchev's authority. Military leaders, along with other influential figures within the party, seized the opportunity to undermine Khrushchev's leadership and eventually succeeded in removing him from power in 1964.

In conclusion, the opposition from military leaders had a profound impact on Khrushchev's rule, particularly during the Cuban Missile

Crisis. Their resistance to Khrushchev's policies of de-Stalinization and military spending cuts, as well as their push for a more confrontational approach, weakened his authority and led to his eventual downfall. This subchapter sheds light on the complex dynamics between Khrushchev and the military establishment and highlights the pivotal role played by this opposition in shaping the course of Soviet history during this period.

The Removal of Khrushchev: Military Factors and Decision-making

The fall of Nikita Khrushchev was a complex event that involved various factors, including military considerations and decision-making processes. This subchapter will delve into the military factors that played a significant role in Khrushchev's removal from power.

One of the key aspects to consider is the Cuban Missile Crisis, which had a profound impact on Khrushchev's rule and ultimately led to his downfall. The crisis exposed Khrushchev's flawed decision-making in deploying nuclear missiles to Cuba without fully considering the potential consequences. This move not only strained Soviet relations with the United States but also triggered a dangerous standoff that brought the world to the brink of nuclear war. Diplomats, historians, and politicians will find valuable insights into how Khrushchev's mishandling of this crisis eroded his political standing and weakened his leadership.

Additionally, Khrushchev's agricultural policies and the subsequent failures of his ambitious Virgin Lands Campaign played a crucial role in his removal from power. By diverting resources and focusing on unproven agricultural methods, Khrushchev neglected other sectors of the Soviet economy, leading to widespread food shortages and discontent among the population. The military, which heavily relied on a well-fed and content populace, began losing faith in Khrushchev's leadership and contributed to his downfall.

Furthermore, Khrushchev's relationship with the Soviet military and its role in his removal cannot be overlooked. Despite his attempts to reform the armed forces and reduce its influence, Khrushchev faced resistance from military leaders who perceived his policies as weakening the Soviet Union's military might. The Cuban Missile Crisis and Khrushchev's subsequent removal were influenced by the military's dissatisfaction with his leadership and decision-making.

Other factors that will be explored in this subchapter include economic reforms, Khrushchev's de-Stalinization campaign, his handling of the Soviet space program, foreign policy decisions, relations with the Eastern Bloc countries, attempts to reform the Soviet political system, and his personality and leadership style. Each of these aspects played a role, directly or indirectly, in Khrushchev's fall from power.

By analyzing the military factors and decision-making processes behind Khrushchev's removal, diplomats, historians, and politicians will gain a deeper understanding of the dynamics that shaped this pivotal moment in Soviet history. This subchapter offers valuable insights into the interplay between military considerations, policies, and the downfall of one of the most significant figures of the Cold War era.

Chapter 4: The Role of Economic Reforms in Khrushchev's Downfall

Khrushchev's Economic Reforms and their Objectives

In the subchapter "Khrushchev's Economic Reforms and their Objectives," we delve into the economic policies implemented by Nikita Khrushchev during his rule, exploring their impact on his eventual downfall. This chapter aims to provide diplomats, historians, and politicians with a comprehensive understanding of the role of economic reforms in Khrushchev's political fate.

Khrushchev's agricultural policies played a significant role in his downfall. The Soviet Union faced numerous challenges in the agricultural sector, with food shortages and inefficiencies plaguing the economy. In an attempt to modernize and increase productivity, Khrushchev introduced the Virgin Lands Campaign, which aimed to cultivate previously uncultivated lands. However, this policy ultimately resulted in decreased yields and exacerbated food shortages, leading to public dissatisfaction and eroding support for Khrushchev.

The relationship between Khrushchev and the Soviet military also played a pivotal role in his removal from power. Khrushchev's attempts to reduce military spending and shift resources towards civilian sectors alienated the military establishment. As a result, high-ranking military officials perceived Khrushchev's policies as a threat to the country's defense capabilities, leading to his removal through a coup.

Economic reforms were not the sole factor in Khrushchev's downfall, but they certainly contributed. Khrushchev's attempts to decentralize economic decision-making and introduce market-oriented reforms faced resistance from entrenched bureaucratic interests. These reforms were seen as a direct challenge to the Soviet political system, creating tensions within the party and among the Soviet elites.

Khrushchev's de-Stalinization campaign also had a profound impact on his political standing. While initially popular, this campaign ultimately alienated conservative party members and Stalin loyalists, who felt threatened by the denouncement of the former leader. This loss of support further weakened Khrushchev's position within the party and contributed to his eventual removal.

Furthermore, Khrushchev's handling of the Soviet space program and foreign policy decisions also played a role in his downfall. The failures of the Soviet space program, particularly the unsuccessful attempt to land a man on the moon, damaged Khrushchev's prestige and undermined his leadership. Additionally, his foreign policy decisions, such as the Cuban Missile Crisis and strained relations with Eastern Bloc countries, further eroded his support base and weakened his position.

Lastly, Khrushchev's personality and leadership style also contributed to his fall from power. His brash and impulsive nature, coupled with his tendency to make public gaffes, damaged his credibility and made him an easy target for his opponents.

In conclusion, this subchapter sheds light on the role of economic reforms in Khrushchev's downfall. By examining his agricultural policies, relationship with the military, handling of the Soviet space program, foreign policy decisions, attempts at political reform, de-Stalinization campaign, and his personality and leadership style, we gain a comprehensive understanding of the factors that led to his removal from power. This analysis provides valuable insights for diplomats, historians, and politicians studying this critical period in Soviet history.

Failures and Challenges of Khrushchev's Economic Policies

The economic policies implemented by Nikita Khrushchev during his rule as the leader of the Soviet Union were riddled with failures and challenges that ultimately contributed to his downfall. This subchapter delves into the intricacies of his economic reforms and the subsequent consequences they had on Khrushchev's political standing, his relationship with the Soviet military, and his removal from power.

One of the key factors that led to Khrushchev's downfall was his agricultural policies. Despite his ambitious goals of increasing agricultural production, his policies proved to be ineffective and even detrimental to the Soviet economy. The collectivization drive resulted in a decline in agricultural output, leading to widespread food shortages and discontent among the population. This failure in addressing food security issues weakened his political standing and eroded public support for his leadership.

Another critical aspect explored in this subchapter is Khrushchev's relationship with the Soviet military. His attempts to reduce military spending and shift resources towards civilian sectors were met with resistance from the military establishment. The Soviet military, which had significant influence and power, perceived these reforms as a threat to their interests and actively worked against Khrushchev's rule. Their opposition played a pivotal role in his removal from power.

Furthermore, Khrushchev's economic reforms, including his de-Stalinization campaign, had a profound impact on his political standing. By denouncing Stalin's policies and initiating a process of political liberalization, Khrushchev faced opposition from hardline conservatives within the Communist Party who were resistant to change. This opposition, combined with economic challenges and the discontent of the military, further weakened his political position and contributed to his downfall.

In addition to his economic policies, Khrushchev's foreign policy decisions also played a significant role in his removal from power. His handling of the Cuban Missile Crisis and his foreign policy ventures, such as the tension with the United States and his strained relationship with the Eastern Bloc countries, further isolated him within the international community and weakened his standing domestically.

Lastly, this subchapter examines Khrushchev's attempt to reform the Soviet political system and his leadership style. His efforts to decentralize power and introduce reforms were met with resistance from party elites who saw it as a threat to their authority. Moreover, his impulsive and erratic leadership style alienated many within the party, contributing to the erosion of his support and ultimately leading to his removal from power.

In conclusion, Khrushchev's economic policies were marred by failures and challenges that ultimately led to his downfall. His agricultural policies, relationship with the military, handling of the Soviet space program, foreign policy decisions, attempts to reform the political system, and leadership style all played significant roles in his removal from power. By examining these factors, we gain a deeper understanding of the complex dynamics that contributed to the unraveling of Khrushchev's rule during the Cuban Missile Crisis.

Economic Factors in Khrushchev's Loss of Power

Nikita Khrushchev's rule was marked by a series of economic challenges that ultimately contributed to his downfall. This subchapter focuses on the economic factors that played a significant role in Khrushchev's loss of power.

One of the key aspects that undermined Khrushchev's rule was his agricultural policies. In an effort to increase agricultural production and catch up with the West, Khrushchev implemented a series of reforms that aimed to modernize the agricultural sector. However, these policies proved to be deeply flawed and had disastrous consequences. The introduction of collective farms and the forced collectivization of agriculture led to a decline in productivity and widespread discontent among farmers. This discontent spread throughout the Soviet Union and eroded Khrushchev's support base.

Furthermore, Khrushchev's relationship with the Soviet military also contributed to his removal from power. Khrushchev's attempts to reduce military spending and shift resources to other sectors of the economy were met with resistance from the military establishment. The Soviet military, a powerful institution with significant influence, saw these policies as a threat to their interests and actively worked against Khrushchev. The military's opposition weakened Khrushchev's position and ultimately played a role in his removal from power.

In addition to agricultural policies and his relationship with the military, economic reforms implemented by Khrushchev also played a part in his downfall. His attempts to decentralize economic decision-making and give more autonomy to regional governments resulted in inefficiencies and economic stagnation. The lack of central planning and coordination led to disparities in economic development among different regions, causing discontent and undermining Khrushchev's authority.

Moreover, Khrushchev's de-Stalinization campaign, aimed at denouncing the brutalities of Stalin's regime, also had economic implications. The campaign created a sense of uncertainty and anxiety among the Soviet elite, who feared that their privileged positions were at risk. This fear of political instability and potential losses led to resistance against Khrushchev's leadership.

Ultimately, although Khrushchev made attempts to reform the Soviet political system and implement economic changes, his policies often resulted in unintended consequences. Combined with his controversial foreign policy decisions, strained relationships with Eastern Bloc countries, and his brash personality and leadership style, these economic factors played a significant role in Khrushchev's loss of power.

In conclusion, Khrushchev's agricultural policies, his relationship with the Soviet military, economic reforms, de-Stalinization campaign, and foreign policy decisions all contributed to his downfall. Understanding these economic factors allows historians, diplomats, and politicians to unravel the complex dynamics that led to Khrushchev's removal from power and gain insights into the broader implications of the Cuban Missile Crisis.

Opposition to Khrushchev's Economic Reforms and its Impact on His Rule

The economic reforms initiated by Nikita Khrushchev during his rule in the Soviet Union were met with significant opposition, ultimately leading to his downfall. This subchapter delves into the reasons behind this opposition and the subsequent impact on his political standing.

Khrushchev's agricultural policies became a focal point of opposition. His attempts to increase agricultural production through the Virgin Lands Campaign and the collectivization of farms faced considerable resistance from the Soviet peasants. The forced collectivization and lack of incentives for the farmers led to a decline in agricultural productivity, causing food shortages and discontent among the population. This opposition to his agricultural policies eroded Khrushchev's support among the people and within the party.

Furthermore, Khrushchev's relationship with the Soviet military played a crucial role in his removal from power. His decision to reduce military spending and focus on developing missiles and nuclear weapons instead encountered strong opposition from the military establishment. The military leaders viewed these reforms as a threat to their influence and prestige, leading to a loss of support for Khrushchev within the military and ultimately contributing to his downfall.

Economic reforms were a double-edged sword for Khrushchev. While he aimed to improve the Soviet economy and raise living standards through his policies, they faced resistance from the conservative elements of the party. These opponents argued that Khrushchev's economic reforms were too radical and undermined the stability of the Soviet system. The opposition from within the party, particularly from influential figures like Leonid Brezhnev, weakened Khrushchev's political standing and set the stage for his removal from power.

Khrushchev's de-Stalinization campaign, which aimed to distance the Soviet Union from the excesses of the Stalin era, also faced significant opposition. The conservative elements of the party, as well as the Soviet military and security apparatus, viewed this campaign as a direct threat to their power and interests. The opposition to de-Stalinization further eroded Khrushchev's political support and contributed to his fall from power.

In addition to domestic opposition, Khrushchev's foreign policy decisions and his handling of the Soviet space program also played a role in his downfall. His involvement in the Cuban Missile Crisis and the subsequent agreement with the United States to remove missiles from Cuba were seen as a sign of weakness by some party members and military leaders. This perception further weakened Khrushchev's position within the party and contributed to his removal from power.

Khrushchev's attempt to reform the Soviet political system, including the decentralization of power and the introduction of more democratic elements, faced resistance from the party hierarchy. The conservative forces within the party saw these reforms as a threat to their control and influence. The opposition to these political reforms played a significant role in Khrushchev's downfall.

Finally, Khrushchev's personality and leadership style also contributed to his fall from power. His impulsive behavior, erratic decision-making, and inability to build strong alliances within the party undermined his authority and led to growing discontent among party members.

In summary, opposition to Khrushchev's economic reforms, including his agricultural policies, his relationship with the Soviet military, his de-Stalinization campaign, and his attempt to reform the Soviet political system, all played a significant role in his removal from power. These opposition forces, combined with his foreign policy decisions, his handling of the Soviet space program, and his leadership style, ultimately led to the downfall of Nikita Khrushchev.

Chapter 5: Khrushchev's De-Stalinization Campaign and Its Impact on His Political Standing

Khrushchev's Efforts to De-Stalinize the Soviet Union

Subchapter: Khrushchev's Efforts to De-Stalinize the Soviet Union

In the turbulent aftermath of Joseph Stalin's death in 1953, Nikita Khrushchev emerged as the Soviet Union's new leader, determined to steer the country away from the oppressive legacy of his predecessor. Khrushchev's de-Stalinization campaign, a bold and controversial endeavor, aimed to transform the Soviet Union both domestically and internationally. This subchapter explores the impact of Khrushchev's de-Stalinization efforts on his political standing, the role of economic reforms, his relationship with the Soviet military and the Eastern Bloc countries, and the influence of his foreign policy decisions and leadership style on his downfall.

Khrushchev understood that the Soviet Union's political system needed to undergo significant changes to regain the trust of its citizens and the international community. He denounced Stalin's cult of personality and initiated a campaign to expose the atrocities committed during his rule. By acknowledging the crimes of the past, Khrushchev sought to rebuild the Soviet Union's reputation and establish a more open and humane society.

However, Khrushchev's de-Stalinization campaign faced resistance from conservative factions within the Soviet Union, particularly the military. His attempts to reduce the influence of the military and implement agricultural policies aimed at increasing food production led to discontent among powerful military leaders and collective farm managers. These policies played a significant role in eroding

Khrushchev's political support, ultimately contributing to his removal from power.

Additionally, Khrushchev's foreign policy decisions, including the Cuban Missile Crisis, strained relations with the United States and other Western powers. While initially seen as a victory, the crisis exposed Khrushchev's impulsive decision-making and undermined his credibility on the international stage.

Furthermore, Khrushchev's attempt to reform the Soviet political system faced resistance from within the Eastern Bloc countries, who feared losing control over their own affairs. This strained relationship with the Eastern Bloc further weakened Khrushchev's position and ultimately led to his removal from power in 1964.

Khrushchev's personality and leadership style also played a significant role in his downfall. His brash and unpredictable nature alienated many within the Soviet leadership, who viewed him as impulsive and lacking the necessary diplomatic skills to navigate the complexities of the Cold War.

In conclusion, Khrushchev's efforts to de-Stalinize the Soviet Union were ambitious and transformative, but ultimately contributed to his fall from power. His agricultural policies, foreign policy decisions, strained relationships with the military and the Eastern Bloc, and his own leadership style all played a role in undermining his political standing. Although his de-Stalinization campaign left a lasting impact on Soviet society, it also highlighted the challenges of implementing radical reforms within a deeply entrenched political system.

Public Reaction and Opposition to De-Stalinization

One of the most significant aspects of Nikita Khrushchev's rule was his campaign of de-Stalinization, which aimed to distance the Soviet Union from the repressive policies of Joseph Stalin. However, this policy was not without its critics, and Khrushchev faced a significant amount of public reaction and opposition to his attempts to reform the Soviet Union.

Khrushchev's de-Stalinization campaign was met with mixed reactions from the Soviet public. On one hand, there were those who welcomed the changes and saw them as a necessary step towards a more open and humane society. These individuals, often intellectuals and artists, saw de-Stalinization as an opportunity for greater freedom of speech and expression.

On the other hand, there were many who were deeply loyal to Stalin and saw Khrushchev's efforts to distance the Soviet Union from his legacy as a betrayal. This group, which included many members of the Communist Party and the Soviet military, viewed de-Stalinization as a threat to the stability and unity of the country.

The opposition to de-Stalinization was particularly strong within the Soviet military. Many high-ranking officers had risen to power under Stalin's leadership and were deeply loyal to him. They saw Khrushchev's attempts to reform the military as an attack on their authority and an attempt to weaken their influence.

Khrushchev also faced opposition from within the Communist Party itself. Many party members were uncomfortable with the idea of openly criticizing Stalin and saw de-Stalinization as a dangerous precedent. They feared that acknowledging Stalin's mistakes would undermine the legitimacy of the party and its leadership.

Overall, while there were those who supported Khrushchev's de-Stalinization campaign, there was significant public reaction and opposition to his efforts. This opposition came from a variety of groups, including loyalists to Stalin, members of the military, and even within the Communist Party itself. These tensions would ultimately play a role in Khrushchev's downfall, as they contributed to a growing sense of instability and division within the Soviet Union.

The Role of De-Stalinization in Khrushchev's Fall from Power

In the tumultuous era of the Cold War, Nikita Khrushchev's rise and fall from power was marked by a series of complex factors and events. One of the key catalysts that contributed to his eventual downfall was his ambitious de-Stalinization campaign and its impact on his political standing within the Soviet Union.

Khrushchev's de-Stalinization campaign, initiated in the mid-1950s, aimed to dismantle the oppressive legacy of Joseph Stalin's regime and usher in a new era of political openness and reform. This campaign involved denouncing Stalin's crimes, releasing political prisoners, and thawing the climate of fear that had gripped the Soviet Union for decades. While these measures were lauded by many within the Soviet Union and the international community, they also created a significant backlash among conservative elements within the Communist Party and the Soviet military.

Diplomats, historians, and politicians must understand the delicate balance that Khrushchev had to maintain as he sought to implement de-Stalinization. On one hand, he had to appease the liberal intellectuals and reformers who supported his initiatives. On the other hand, he had to navigate the treacherous waters of the Soviet military and the conservative party elite, who viewed his reforms as a threat to their power and the stability of the regime.

Khrushchev's de-Stalinization campaign also had unintended consequences that further eroded his political standing. As the revelations of Stalin's crimes became public, it sparked a wave of discontent among the Soviet population who had lived under his repressive rule. This newfound freedom of expression resulted in widespread criticism and disillusionment with the Soviet system, as well as demands for further political and economic reforms.

Furthermore, Khrushchev's attempts to distance himself from Stalin's legacy led to a loss of ideological cohesion within the Communist Party. The once-unified party splintered into factions, with some members embracing Khrushchev's reforms while others vehemently opposed them. This internal division weakened Khrushchev's position and made him vulnerable to political maneuvering by his opponents.

In conclusion, Khrushchev's de-Stalinization campaign played a crucial role in his fall from power. While it initially garnered support from liberals and reformers, it also alienated conservative elements within the party and the military. The unintended consequences of the campaign, such as public discontent and ideological divisions, further weakened Khrushchev's position. Ultimately, his ambitious efforts to dismantle Stalin's legacy ultimately became a double-edged sword that contributed to his downfall. This chapter will delve deeper into the complexities of Khrushchev's de-Stalinization campaign and its impact on his political standing, providing valuable insights for diplomats, historians, and politicians alike.

Criticisms and Repercussions of Khrushchev's De-Stalinization Policies

Khrushchev's de-Stalinization policies, aimed at dismantling the cult of personality surrounding Joseph Stalin, faced significant criticisms and had far-reaching repercussions during his rule. This subchapter explores the various aspects of these policies and their impact on Khrushchev's downfall, shedding light on their significance for diplomats, historians, and politicians studying the era.

One of the major criticisms of Khrushchev's de-Stalinization campaign was its effect on the role of the Cuban Missile Crisis in his fall from power. By publicly denouncing Stalin's actions and policies, Khrushchev inadvertently weakened his own position within the Soviet leadership, making it easier for his opponents to question his judgment during the crisis. This chapter delves into the intricacies of the crisis and its connection to Khrushchev's de-Stalinization policies, providing valuable insights for diplomats and historians interested in understanding the sequence of events that led to his removal.

Furthermore, Khrushchev's agricultural policies and their impact on his downfall are examined in this subchapter. His attempts to modernize and industrialize Soviet agriculture were met with resistance and resulted in significant shortcomings, leading to food shortages and discontent among the population. By analyzing these policies and their repercussions, this chapter offers valuable lessons for politicians seeking to understand the importance of maintaining a sustainable and productive agricultural sector.

The subchapter also explores Khrushchev's relationship with the Soviet military and its role in his removal from power. Khrushchev's attempts to reduce the military's influence and shift resources towards civilian sectors were met with resistance and criticism from within the military establishment. Understanding this dynamic is crucial for historians and politicians studying power struggles within authoritarian regimes and the consequences of challenging military interests.

Additionally, the economic reforms implemented by Khrushchev and their role in his downfall are discussed. While some of these reforms showed promise, others were met with skepticism and resistance. By examining the successes and failures of these reforms, this chapter offers valuable insights for diplomats and politicians seeking to navigate economic transformations while maintaining political stability.

Lastly, this subchapter delves into Khrushchev's foreign policy decisions and their role in his downfall. From his handling of the Soviet space program to his relationships with Eastern Bloc countries, Khrushchev's foreign policy choices had far-reaching consequences. By analyzing these decisions, historians and politicians can gain a deeper understanding of the complexities of Cold War-era diplomacy and its impact on domestic politics.

In conclusion, this subchapter on the criticisms and repercussions of Khrushchev's de-Stalinization policies provides a comprehensive analysis of the factors contributing to his downfall. It offers valuable insights for diplomats, historians, and politicians interested in understanding the role of the Cuban Missile Crisis, agricultural policies, military dynamics, economic reforms, foreign policy decisions, and Khrushchev's leadership style in shaping the fate of his rule.

Chapter 6: Khrushchev's Handling of the Soviet Space Program and Its Influence on His Fall from Power

Khrushchev's Prioritization of the Space Program

Subchapter: Khrushchev's Prioritization of the Space Program

In the midst of the political turmoil and internal struggles faced by Nikita Khrushchev during his rule, one of the key aspects that stood out was his prioritization of the Soviet space program. Khrushchev's emphasis on space exploration and his determination to outpace the United States in this domain had a profound impact on his political standing and ultimately contributed to his downfall.

At the height of the Cold War, the space race between the Soviet Union and the United States was not only a technological competition but also a symbol of ideological superiority. Khrushchev believed that achieving significant milestones in space exploration would demonstrate the superiority of the Soviet socialist system, thereby bolstering his own image and consolidating his power. As a result, he allocated substantial resources and attention to the development of the Soviet space program.

While Khrushchev's focus on space exploration may have seemed justified in terms of propaganda and international prestige, this prioritization came at the expense of other critical areas such as agriculture and economic reforms. The Soviet Union, already grappling with agricultural inefficiencies, suffered greatly due to the diversion of resources and attention away from the agricultural sector. This negligence exacerbated food shortages and contributed to widespread dissatisfaction among the Soviet population, ultimately eroding support for Khrushchev's regime.

Furthermore, Khrushchev's close association with the Soviet military and their involvement in the space program played a significant role in his removal from power. The military, resentful of Khrushchev's attempts to reduce their influence in policymaking, viewed his prioritization of space exploration as a distraction from military modernization efforts. This tension culminated in a power struggle, with the military aligning with Khrushchev's political opponents to undermine his authority and ultimately force his removal.

Khrushchev's handling of the space program also had international ramifications. His bold decision to install nuclear missiles in Cuba during the Cuban Missile Crisis was a direct consequence of his desire to secure a strategic advantage in the space race. However, this decision brought the world perilously close to nuclear war, tarnishing Khrushchev's reputation on the international stage and further isolating him from his Eastern Bloc allies.

In conclusion, while Khrushchev's prioritization of the space program may have been driven by a desire for political gain and international prestige, it ultimately contributed to his downfall. Neglecting critical areas such as agriculture, alienating the Soviet military, and making ill-advised foreign policy decisions all played a role in eroding his political standing and ultimately led to his removal from power. Khrushchev's focus on the space program serves as a cautionary tale, highlighting the importance of balancing priorities and addressing the needs of the population when making policy decisions.

Achievements and Setbacks in the Soviet Space Program

The Soviet Union's space program achieved remarkable milestones during the tenure of Nikita Khrushchev, but it also faced significant setbacks that had far-reaching consequences. This subchapter explores the achievements and setbacks in the Soviet space program and their influence on Khrushchev's fall from power.

Under Khrushchev's leadership, the Soviet Union made groundbreaking achievements in space exploration. In 1957, they launched the world's first artificial satellite, Sputnik, which marked the beginning of the Space Age. This triumph demonstrated the Soviet Union's technological capabilities and ignited the space race with the United States. In 1961, Yuri Gagarin became the first human to orbit the Earth, a momentous achievement that further solidified the Soviet Union's superiority in space exploration.

However, the Soviet space program also encountered significant setbacks. In 1960, the launch of the Korabl-Sputnik 2, carrying the dog Laika, ended in tragedy as the spacecraft failed to reenter the Earth's atmosphere safely. This incident sparked international outcry and raised ethical concerns about animal welfare. The subsequent failures of various lunar missions, including the Luna 2 and Luna 15, diminished the Soviet Union's prestige in the space race.

These setbacks in the space program had a profound impact on Khrushchev's political standing. Despite the initial successes, the failures eroded confidence in his leadership and contributed to a perception of incompetence. The United States, on the other hand, capitalized on these setbacks and launched successful missions, such as the Apollo program, which culminated in the moon landing in 1969. The Soviet Union's inability to match these accomplishments further weakened Khrushchev's position domestically and internationally.

Moreover, the space program's setbacks also exposed underlying issues within the Soviet system. Khrushchev's attempt to prioritize quantity over quality in space exploration, driven by his desire to showcase Soviet achievements, resulted in rushed and flawed missions. This highlighted the shortcomings of Khrushchev's economic reforms and his failure to allocate sufficient resources to the space program.

In conclusion, while the Soviet space program achieved remarkable milestones under Khrushchev's rule, the setbacks it faced had a significant influence on his fall from power. The failures damaged his reputation and the Soviet Union's standing in the international arena. Additionally, these setbacks revealed deeper issues within the Soviet system, highlighting the flaws in Khrushchev's leadership style and economic policies. Ultimately, the achievements and setbacks in the Soviet space program played a crucial role in Khrushchev's downfall.

Public Perception and International Reactions to Soviet Space Exploration

One of the most significant aspects of Nikita Khrushchev's rule was the Soviet Union's advancement in space exploration. The Soviet space program, led by Khrushchev, captivated the world and had far-reaching implications for public perception and international relations. This subchapter will delve into the public's reaction to Soviet space exploration and its impact on Khrushchev's political standing, as well as the international community's response.

Khrushchev's ambitious space program aimed to showcase Soviet technological superiority and challenge the United States' dominance in space. The launch of Sputnik in 1957, the world's first artificial satellite, astounded the global audience and demonstrated the Soviet Union's scientific prowess. It caused a wave of awe and apprehension among diplomats, historians, and politicians, who recognized the potential military implications of this technological feat.

The subsequent achievements of Soviet space exploration, including the first human spaceflight by Yuri Gagarin in 1961, further enhanced the Soviet Union's international prestige. However, Khrushchev's handling of these accomplishments was not always successful in bolstering his political standing. While the public marveled at these achievements,

Khrushchev faced criticism for diverting resources to the space program instead of addressing pressing domestic issues.

Internationally, the Soviet space program triggered a race for space dominance between the United States and the Soviet Union, known as the Space Race. This competition had significant political and ideological implications. The United States, alarmed by the Soviet Union's advancements, intensified its own space program, which ultimately led to the Apollo moon landing in 1969. This race further strained the already tense Cold War relations between the two superpowers.

Moreover, Khrushchev's handling of the space program had a profound impact on his foreign policy decisions and relationship with the Eastern Bloc countries. The success of Soviet space exploration bolstered Khrushchev's confidence, leading him to adopt a more assertive foreign policy stance. This, however, alienated some Eastern Bloc countries, who viewed Khrushchev's actions as overly aggressive and destabilizing.

In conclusion, public perception and international reactions to Soviet space exploration played a crucial role in Khrushchev's downfall. While the achievements of the Soviet space program initially enhanced Khrushchev's political standing domestically and internationally, they also brought about challenges and criticisms. The Space Race intensified Cold War tensions, and Khrushchev's handling of the program influenced his foreign policy decisions and strained his relationship with Eastern Bloc countries. Ultimately, the perception of Khrushchev's prioritization of the space program over other domestic issues contributed to his removal from power.

The Role of the Space Program in Khrushchev's Downfall

In the tumultuous era of the Cold War, the Soviet Union's space program emerged as a powerful tool for propaganda and technological prowess.

However, it also played a significant role in the downfall of Nikita Khrushchev, the leader of the Soviet Union during the Cuban Missile Crisis. This subchapter explores the intricate relationship between Khrushchev's handling of the space program and his ultimate removal from power.

Under Khrushchev's rule, the Soviet Union made remarkable advancements in space exploration. The launch of Sputnik, the first artificial satellite, in 1957, and Yuri Gagarin's historic manned spaceflight in 1961 demonstrated the Soviet Union's scientific superiority to the world. Khrushchev cleverly used these achievements to bolster national pride and project the image of a progressive superpower.

However, Khrushchev's obsession with the space program came at a cost. As he poured substantial resources into space exploration, other crucial sectors like agriculture and industry suffered. Khrushchev's agricultural policies, including the ill-conceived Virgin Lands Campaign, failed to yield the expected results, leading to food shortages and discontent among the Soviet population. This mismanagement eroded Khrushchev's popular support and weakened his political standing.

Furthermore, Khrushchev's relationship with the Soviet military was strained. The military leadership resented his focus on the space program, viewing it as a drain on resources that could be better utilized for defense purposes. Khrushchev's inability to balance the demands of the military and the space program undermined his authority and provided ammunition to his opponents within the Soviet political elite.

Economic reforms were another crucial aspect of Khrushchev's downfall, and the space program played a role in this too. Khrushchev's push for decentralization and the introduction of regional economic councils disrupted the central planning system. The resources allocated to the space program diverted attention and funding from essential economic sectors, exacerbating existing economic problems and contributing to his eventual removal from power.

Moreover, Khrushchev's de-Stalinization campaign, which aimed to distance the Soviet Union from the repressive era of Stalin, faced significant opposition from conservative elements within the party. The space program, with its emphasis on technological progress and innovation, symbolized Khrushchev's vision of a new Soviet Union, free from the shackles of Stalinism. This clash of ideologies further eroded Khrushchev's political support and paved the way for his downfall.

In conclusion, while the Soviet space program brought glory and international recognition to the Soviet Union, it also played a significant role in Khrushchev's downfall. His mismanagement of resources, strained relationship with the military, economic reforms, and clash with conservative elements contributed to his removal from power. The space program became a symbol of Khrushchev's ambitious yet flawed leadership style, ultimately undermining his political standing and hastening his downfall.

Chapter 7: Khrushchev's Foreign Policy Decisions and Their Role in His Downfall

Khrushchev's Foreign Policy Objectives

One of the key aspects that contributed to the fall of Nikita Khrushchev was his foreign policy decisions. Throughout his rule, Khrushchev pursued various objectives in his international relations, but many of these decisions had unintended consequences that ultimately led to his downfall.

First and foremost, Khrushchev aimed to challenge the United States and assert Soviet dominance on the global stage. This objective became evident during the Cuban Missile Crisis, a pivotal event that unraveled Khrushchev's rule. Seeking to counterbalance American influence in the Western Hemisphere, Khrushchev deployed nuclear missiles to Cuba, triggering a dangerous standoff with the United States. This aggressive move led to a global crisis and damaged Khrushchev's credibility, further alienating him from his own military and political allies.

Furthermore, Khrushchev's foreign policy decisions were often intertwined with his agricultural policies, which ultimately contributed to his downfall. Khrushchev implemented ambitious agricultural reforms, aiming to increase food production and improve living standards for Soviet citizens. However, these policies failed to yield the desired results, leading to widespread food shortages and discontent among the population. The agricultural failures undermined Khrushchev's leadership, as his inability to provide for his people eroded support from key factions within the Soviet Union.

Khrushchev's relationship with the Soviet military also played a significant role in his removal from power. Despite his attempts to modernize and streamline the military, Khrushchev faced resistance from conservative factions within the armed forces. His foreign policy decisions, particularly the Cuban Missile Crisis, highlighted a disconnect between Khrushchev and the military leadership. This strained relationship weakened Khrushchev's position and provided an opportunity for his political opponents to seize power.

Moreover, Khrushchev's attempts at economic reforms also contributed to his downfall. While he sought to decentralize economic decision-making and increase consumer goods production, these reforms created economic inefficiencies and failed to deliver the expected results. The economic stagnation, coupled with his agricultural policies, further eroded Khrushchev's support base and weakened his political standing.

In addition to these factors, Khrushchev's de-Stalinization campaign and his handling of the Soviet space program also played a role in his fall from power. His denunciation of Stalin's crimes and efforts to distance the Soviet Union from its dark past sparked controversy and opposition from conservative elements within the Communist Party. Furthermore, Khrushchev's mishandling of the Soviet space program, including several high-profile failures, undermined his image as a competent leader and contributed to a loss of confidence from his colleagues.

Overall, Khrushchev's foreign policy decisions, intertwined with his agricultural policies, relationship with the Soviet military, economic reforms, de-Stalinization campaign, and handling of the space program, all played a role in his downfall. While his objectives were ambitious, Khrushchev's inability to effectively manage these various aspects of his rule ultimately led to his removal from power.

Key Foreign Policy Decisions and their Consequences

The Cuban Missile Crisis, a pivotal event in the Cold War, played a significant role in the fall of Nikita Khrushchev. This subchapter explores the consequences of Khrushchev's key foreign policy decisions and sheds light on the multiple factors leading to his removal from power. Addressing diplomats, historians, and politicians, we delve into the intricate details of Khrushchev's downfall to provide a comprehensive understanding of this historical period.

Khrushchev's agricultural policies were instrumental in his political demise. His ambitious plans to increase agricultural production through collectivization and the Virgin Lands Campaign proved disastrous. These policies resulted in widespread food shortages, undermining his popularity and eroding support within the Soviet Union.

Furthermore, Khrushchev's relationship with the Soviet military played a crucial role in his removal from power. His attempts to reduce military spending and shift the focus towards peaceful coexistence with the West faced fierce resistance from military leaders. Their opposition weakened Khrushchev's authority and contributed to his downfall.

Economic reforms also played a significant role in Khrushchev's downfall. His attempts to decentralize the economy and introduce market-oriented reforms clashed with the entrenched Soviet bureaucracy. This resistance, coupled with the failures of his agricultural policies, created a sense of economic instability and further eroded his political standing.

Khrushchev's de-Stalinization campaign, aimed at denouncing the excesses of the Stalin era, had a profound impact on his political standing. While it initially garnered support among intellectuals and liberals, it alienated conservative elements within the Soviet leadership, who viewed it as a threat to their power. This division weakened Khrushchev's position and contributed to his eventual removal.

Additionally, Khrushchev's handling of the Soviet space program influenced his fall from power. Despite early successes, his ambitious space goals and costly missions strained the Soviet economy. Failures such as the Bay of Pigs invasion and the U-2 spy plane incident tarnished the Soviet Union's international reputation and undermined Khrushchev's standing.

Khrushchev's foreign policy decisions, including the Cuban Missile Crisis, further weakened his position. The crisis, a standoff between the United States and the Soviet Union over the placement of nuclear missiles in Cuba, exposed Khrushchev's miscalculations and diplomatic blunders. The resolution of the crisis, with the removal of Soviet missiles from Cuba, was seen by many as a Soviet defeat, diminishing Khrushchev's prestige.

Moreover, Khrushchev's relationships with Eastern Bloc countries strained his authority. His attempts to exert control and pressure on these nations, particularly during the Hungarian Revolution of 1956, led to resentment and a loss of support within the Bloc. This fracture weakened Khrushchev's position and contributed to his eventual removal.

Furthermore, Khrushchev's attempts to reform the Soviet political system faced significant resistance. His efforts to decentralize power and increase local autonomy threatened the entrenched Soviet bureaucracy and conservative elements within the party. These opponents capitalized on the economic instability and failures of his policies, ultimately leading to his downfall.

Lastly, Khrushchev's personality and leadership style played a significant role in his fall from power. His erratic behavior, including his famous shoe-banging incident at the United Nations, diminished his credibility on the international stage and weakened his position domestically. His brash and impulsive decision-making alienated key allies and further undermined his authority.

In conclusion, the fall of Nikita Khrushchev was the result of a complex interplay of factors, including the role of the Cuban Missile Crisis, his agricultural policies, his relationship with the Soviet military, economic reforms, de-Stalinization, the Soviet space program, foreign policy decisions, Eastern Bloc relations, attempts at political reform, and his personality and leadership style. This subchapter provides a comprehensive analysis of these key foreign policy decisions and their consequences, shedding light on a pivotal period in Soviet history.

International Reactions and Criticisms of Khrushchev's Foreign Policy

Khrushchev's foreign policy decisions during his rule faced intense scrutiny and criticism from the international community. This subchapter explores the various reactions and criticisms that arose in response to Khrushchev's approach to global affairs.

One of the most significant events that unfolded during Khrushchev's tenure was the Cuban Missile Crisis, which had far-reaching implications for his rule. Diplomats, historians, and politicians have since analyzed how this crisis contributed to his downfall. The book highlights the role played by Khrushchev's risky gamble in placing missiles in Cuba, which brought the world to the brink of nuclear war. The international community's response to this crisis and their subsequent criticism of Khrushchev's handling of the situation are examined in detail.

Another aspect of Khrushchev's foreign policy that drew widespread criticism was his relationship with the Eastern Bloc countries. The book delves into the impact of his strained relationship with these nations on his removal from power. The audience is provided with insights into the complex dynamics that existed between Khrushchev and the Eastern Bloc, shedding light on how these tensions contributed to his downfall.

Furthermore, Khrushchev's attempts to reform the Soviet political system also faced international criticism. The book explores the role of these reform efforts in his downfall, examining how they were perceived by diplomats, historians, and politicians from other countries. The audience gains a deeper understanding of the challenges Khrushchev encountered as he sought to reshape the Soviet political landscape.

Khrushchev's foreign policy decisions, such as his handling of the Soviet space program, also come under scrutiny. The book analyzes how these decisions influenced his fall from power and the international reactions they elicited. The audience gains a comprehensive understanding of the interplay between Khrushchev's foreign policy choices and their impact on his political standing.

Overall, this subchapter provides diplomats, historians, and politicians with a nuanced exploration of the international reactions and criticisms of Khrushchev's foreign policy decisions. By examining the Cuban Missile Crisis, his relationship with the Eastern Bloc, his attempts at political reform, and his handling of the Soviet space program, the book sheds light on how these factors collectively contributed to his downfall.

The Impact of Foreign Policy on Khrushchev's Loss of Power

The Cuban Missile Crisis: Unraveling Khrushchev's Rule

Chapter 4: The Impact of Foreign Policy on Khrushchev's Loss of Power

Introduction:

In this subchapter, we will delve into the significant influence of foreign policy on Nikita Khrushchev's downfall. As diplomats, historians, and politicians, it is crucial to understand the multifaceted factors contributing to the demise of a leader. Khrushchev's foreign policy decisions played a pivotal role in shaping his political standing and eventual removal from power.

1. The Cuban Missile Crisis and the Fall of Khrushchev:

The Cuban Missile Crisis marked a turning point in Khrushchev's rule. His decision to install nuclear missiles in Cuba without consulting his advisors or allies strained his relations with the Soviet military and the Eastern Bloc countries. This miscalculated move not only escalated tensions with the United States but also portrayed Khrushchev as a reckless leader, eroding his political standing.

2. Khrushchev's Agricultural Policies and Their Impact on His Downfall:

Khrushchev's ambitious agricultural policies, particularly the Virgin Lands Campaign, aimed to boost Soviet food production. However, the failure of these policies, coupled with his inability to adequately address agricultural challenges, led to food shortages and a decline in his popularity among the Soviet people. This discontent further weakened his political position.

3. Khrushchev's Relationship with the Soviet Military and Its Role in His Removal from Power:

Khrushchev's strained relationship with the Soviet military, exacerbated by his handling of the Cuban Missile Crisis, was a significant factor in his removal from power. His attempt to downsize the military and shift focus to nuclear weapons and missile technology faced strong opposition from the military establishment, ultimately undermining his authority.

4. Economic Reforms and Their Role in Khrushchev's Downfall:

Khrushchev's economic reforms, such as the shift towards consumer goods production and decentralization of economic decision-making, faced resistance from the party's hardliners. The failure to achieve desired economic outcomes weakened Khrushchev's position, as his opponents perceived these reforms as detrimental to the Soviet economy.

5. De-Stalinization Campaign and Its Impact on Khrushchev's Political Standing:

Khrushchev's de-Stalinization campaign aimed to distance the Soviet Union from the repressive policies of Joseph Stalin. However, this campaign faced resistance from conservative forces within the party and Eastern Bloc countries who still revered Stalin. Khrushchev's attempts to dismantle the cult of personality surrounding Stalin further eroded his support base.

6. Khrushchev's Foreign Policy Decisions and Their Role in His Downfall:

Khrushchev's foreign policy decisions, such as the Cuban Missile Crisis and his aggressive stance towards the West, strained Soviet relations with the United States and its allies. These decisions led to increased international tensions, damaged the Soviet Union's reputation, and portrayed Khrushchev as an unpredictable leader, ultimately contributing to his removal from power.

Conclusion:

Khrushchev's foreign policy decisions, including the Cuban Missile Crisis, his agricultural policies, strained relationship with the military, economic reforms, de-Stalinization campaign, and handling of the Soviet space program, played a significant role in his loss of power. By analyzing these factors, diplomats, historians, and politicians can gain a comprehensive understanding of the complexities of leadership and the impact of foreign policy decisions on a leader's downfall.

Chapter 8: Khrushchev's Relationship with the Eastern Bloc Countries and Its Impact on His Removal from Power

Khrushchev's Attempts to Maintain Control over the Eastern Bloc

In his quest to maintain control over the Eastern Bloc, Nikita Khrushchev embarked on a series of strategies and policies that shaped the course of his rule and ultimately contributed to his downfall. This subchapter explores the intricacies of Khrushchev's relationship with the Eastern Bloc countries and the impact it had on his removal from power.

Khrushchev's attempts to maintain control over the Eastern Bloc were primarily driven by his desire to solidify Soviet dominance in the region and prevent any potential threat to his rule. Aware of the fragility of the Soviet empire, Khrushchev sought to establish close ties with the Eastern Bloc countries, often employing a mix of coercion and economic incentives. This approach aimed to ensure their loyalty and prevent any dissent that could undermine his rule.

However, Khrushchev's efforts were met with mixed results. While some Eastern Bloc countries, such as East Germany and Poland, remained staunch allies, others like Hungary and Czechoslovakia began to demonstrate signs of discontent. Khrushchev's handling of the Hungarian Revolution in 1956, for instance, marked a turning point in his relationship with the Eastern Bloc. The brutal suppression of the uprising strained his ties with the countries of the region and eroded their trust in Soviet leadership.

Furthermore, Khrushchev's attempts to reform the Soviet political system and his de-Stalinization campaign also impacted his relationship with the Eastern Bloc. These initiatives, aimed at reducing the cult of personality and promoting a more open political environment, were met with suspicion and resistance from conservative elements within the Eastern Bloc countries. They viewed these reforms as a threat to their own positions of power and as potential Western influence seeping into their territories.

Khrushchev's personality and leadership style further complicated his relationship with the Eastern Bloc. His impulsive and unpredictable nature often created uncertainty among the Eastern Bloc leaders, making it difficult for them to gauge his intentions accurately. This lack of trust and confidence in Khrushchev's leadership ultimately contributed to his removal from power.

In conclusion, Khrushchev's attempts to maintain control over the Eastern Bloc were marked by a delicate balance of coercion, economic incentives, and political reforms. However, factors such as the Hungarian Revolution, his de-Stalinization campaign, and his unpredictable leadership style strained his relationship with the Eastern Bloc and ultimately played a significant role in his downfall. Understanding these dynamics sheds light on the complex interplay between Khrushchev's domestic and international policies.

Tensions and Discord within the Eastern Bloc

The Cuban Missile Crisis was a turning point in the history of the Cold War, and it played a significant role in the fall of Nikita Khrushchev. This subchapter explores the tensions and discord that existed within the Eastern Bloc during this critical period. It sheds light on the intricate relationships between Khrushchev, the Soviet military, and the Eastern Bloc countries, and how these dynamics ultimately led to his removal from power.

Khrushchev's agricultural policies had a profound impact on his downfall. His ambitious plans to modernize and increase agricultural production fell short, leading to food shortages and discontent within the Soviet Union. This discontent was mirrored in the Eastern Bloc countries, where agricultural reforms were met with resistance and skepticism. The failure of these policies eroded Khrushchev's political standing, making him vulnerable to opposition from within his own ranks.

Khrushchev's relationship with the Soviet military also played a crucial role in his removal from power. The Cuban Missile Crisis highlighted the tensions between Khrushchev's desire for peaceful coexistence and the military's preference for a more confrontational approach. This discord weakened Khrushchev's authority and provided an opportunity for his opponents to challenge his leadership.

Economic reforms were another factor that contributed to Khrushchev's downfall. While he implemented policies aimed at increasing economic efficiency, they often resulted in unintended consequences. The Eastern Bloc countries, already burdened by economic struggles, were resistant to these reforms, exacerbating the existing tensions and divisions within the bloc.

Khrushchev's de-Stalinization campaign, an attempt to distance the Soviet Union from the excesses of Stalin's rule, also had an impact on his political standing. While some within the Eastern Bloc welcomed this shift, others saw it as a betrayal of the socialist ideals they had embraced. This further strained Khrushchev's relationships with these countries, weakening his position and making him susceptible to opposition.

Khrushchev's foreign policy decisions, including his handling of the Soviet space program and his attempts to expand Soviet influence abroad, also contributed to his downfall. These decisions often strained relations with the Eastern Bloc countries, as they felt overshadowed by the Soviet Union's global ambitions. This further eroded Khrushchev's support within the bloc and provided ammunition for his opponents.

Overall, tensions and discord within the Eastern Bloc played a crucial role in Khrushchev's removal from power. The agricultural policies, relationship with the military, economic reforms, de-Stalinization campaign, foreign policy decisions, and his attempt to reform the Soviet political system all contributed to the deterioration of his political standing. Additionally, Khrushchev's personality and leadership style, characterized by his impulsive and erratic behavior, further alienated him from his allies. Understanding these dynamics is essential for diplomats, historians, and politicians seeking to unravel the complexities of the Cuban Missile Crisis and its impact on Khrushchev's rule.

Opposition from Eastern Bloc Countries and its Role in Khrushchev's Downfall

In the turbulent era of the Cold War, Nikita Khrushchev's reign as the leader of the Soviet Union was marked by a series of challenges and controversies. Among the many factors contributing to his eventual downfall, the opposition from Eastern Bloc countries played a significant role. This subchapter will shed light on the intricate dynamics within the Eastern Bloc and how they ultimately contributed to Khrushchev's removal from power.

Khrushchev's attempts to reform the Soviet political system, particularly his policy of de-Stalinization, was met with staunch resistance from Eastern Bloc countries, who saw this as a threat to their own regimes. The Eastern Bloc, under Soviet influence, had adopted Stalinist policies, and any deviation from this ideology was seen as a betrayal. As a result, leaders from countries such as East Germany, Poland, and Hungary openly criticized Khrushchev's reforms. Their opposition intensified as Khrushchev's reforms led to political unrest and demands for greater independence within their own borders.

Furthermore, Khrushchev's foreign policy decisions also strained his relationship with the Eastern Bloc. The Cuban Missile Crisis in particular highlighted the differing approaches between Khrushchev and his Eastern Bloc counterparts. While Khrushchev's decision to place nuclear missiles in Cuba was seen as a show of strength against the United States, it caused anxiety and unease among Eastern Bloc leaders. They feared that this provocative move would escalate tensions and potentially lead to a nuclear war, jeopardizing their own security.

Khrushchev's handling of the Soviet space program also contributed to his downfall. While the successful launch of Sputnik had initially bolstered his image, subsequent failures and setbacks tarnished his reputation. Eastern Bloc countries, particularly those aiming to rival the United States in space exploration, viewed these failures as a reflection of Khrushchev's incompetence and inability to deliver on his promises.

The opposition from Eastern Bloc countries, both politically and ideologically, weakened Khrushchev's position within the Soviet Union. The combination of resistance to his reforms, disagreement over foreign policy decisions, and disappointment with his handling of the space program created a sense of disillusionment among his Eastern Bloc allies.

In conclusion, the opposition from Eastern Bloc countries played a crucial role in Khrushchev's downfall. The resistance to his reforms, disagreement over foreign policy decisions, and disappointment with his handling of the space program all contributed to the erosion of his support and ultimately led to his removal from power. Understanding the intricate dynamics within the Eastern Bloc is essential for diplomats, historians, and politicians seeking to comprehend the complexities of the Cold War era and the factors that shaped Khrushchev's rule.

The Eastern Bloc's Influence on Khrushchev's Removal from Power

One of the key factors contributing to Nikita Khrushchev's removal from power was his relationship with the Eastern Bloc countries. The Eastern Bloc, comprised of the Soviet Union and its satellite states in

Eastern Europe, played a significant role in shaping Khrushchev's downfall.

Khrushchev's attempt to reform the Soviet political system, known as the "Secret Speech" in 1956, deeply impacted his relationship with the Eastern Bloc. In this speech, Khrushchev denounced the excesses and crimes committed under Stalin's rule, which caused a ripple effect throughout the Eastern Bloc. Several Eastern Bloc leaders, who owed their positions to Stalin's support, were deeply offended and threatened by Khrushchev's de-Stalinization campaign. This led to a deterioration in relations between Khrushchev and his Eastern Bloc counterparts, creating a significant obstacle for him in maintaining his power base.

Furthermore, Khrushchev's foreign policy decisions, particularly his handling of the Cuban Missile Crisis, also strained his relationship with the Eastern Bloc. The crisis, which brought the world to the brink of nuclear war, highlighted Khrushchev's reckless decision-making and lack of consultation with his Eastern Bloc allies. Many Eastern Bloc leaders felt marginalized and ignored by Khrushchev's unilateral actions, causing further resentment and distrust towards him.

Economic reforms implemented by Khrushchev also had consequences for his relationship with the Eastern Bloc. Khrushchev's agricultural policies, including the Virgin Lands Campaign and the emphasis on corn production, had a disastrous impact on the Soviet economy. These policies were exported to the Eastern Bloc countries, causing similar economic hardships. The Eastern Bloc leaders, already frustrated with Khrushchev's political reforms, now faced economic challenges that further eroded their support for him.

Moreover, Khrushchev's personality and leadership style played a significant role in his downfall. His brash and impulsive nature, coupled with his tendency to alienate allies, strained his relationship with the Eastern Bloc. Khrushchev's abrasive style of diplomacy often clashed with the more cautious and conservative leaders of the Eastern Bloc, leading to a breakdown in communication and cooperation.

In conclusion, the Eastern Bloc's influence on Khrushchev's removal from power cannot be underestimated. His strained relationship with the Eastern Bloc leaders due to his de-Stalinization campaign, foreign policy decisions, economic reforms, and leadership style all contributed to his downfall. The Eastern Bloc's dissatisfaction and resentment towards Khrushchev ultimately led to his removal from power, marking the end of an era in Soviet leadership.

Chapter 9: Khrushchev's Attempt to Reform the Soviet Political System and Its Role in His Downfall

Khrushchev's Efforts to Reform the Political System

Nikita Khrushchev, the enigmatic leader of the Soviet Union during the turbulent years of the Cold War, is often remembered for his daring actions and bold decisions. One of the most significant aspects of his rule was his relentless drive to reform the political system of the Soviet Union. Khrushchev recognized the need for change and was determined to modernize the Soviet state.

Khrushchev's attempt to reform the political system was born out of his desire to distance himself from the legacy of his predecessor, Joseph Stalin. He launched a campaign of de-Stalinization, which aimed to dismantle the oppressive and totalitarian regime that had characterized Stalin's rule. Khrushchev denounced Stalin's cult of personality and sought to create a more open and transparent political environment.

Under Khrushchev's leadership, the Soviet Union witnessed a period of significant economic reforms. His agricultural policies, known as the Virgin Lands campaign, aimed to increase food production by cultivating previously unused land. However, these policies proved to be ill-conceived and ultimately led to a decline in agricultural output. This failure had a detrimental impact on Khrushchev's popularity and played a significant role in his downfall.

Khrushchev's relationship with the Soviet military was also a key factor in his removal from power. Despite his efforts to modernize and strengthen the military, he faced opposition from the military establishment. The Cuban Missile Crisis, a pivotal moment during his rule, highlighted the tensions between Khrushchev and the military. His decision to place nuclear missiles in Cuba without consulting military commanders strained their relationship and eroded his authority.

Furthermore, Khrushchev's handling of the Soviet space program had a profound influence on his fall from power. While he championed Soviet achievements in space, such as the launch of the first manned satellite, his ambitious goals often led to unrealistic expectations. Failures in the space program, including the disastrous launch of the lunar probe, further damaged Khrushchev's standing and undermined his credibility.

In addition to his domestic policies, Khrushchev's foreign policy decisions played a significant role in his downfall. His attempts to thaw the Cold War tensions with the United States were met with mixed results. The Cuban Missile Crisis, in particular, showcased Khrushchev's miscalculations and brinkmanship, which diminished his international standing.

Khrushchev's attempts to reform the Soviet political system ultimately contributed to his downfall. His efforts to decentralize power and promote a more collective leadership style were met with resistance from conservative elements within the Soviet Union. The Eastern Bloc countries, in particular, felt threatened by Khrushchev's reforms and viewed them as a challenge to their own authority.

Finally, Khrushchev's personality and leadership style also played a role in his fall from power. His brash and impulsive nature, coupled with his tendency to make grandiose promises, alienated many within the Soviet leadership. His unpredictable behavior undermined his credibility and led to a loss of confidence from his colleagues.

In conclusion, Khrushchev's efforts to reform the political system of the Soviet Union were ambitious and well-intentioned. However, a combination of factors, including his agricultural policies, strained relationship with the military, economic failures, foreign policy decisions, and leadership style, ultimately led to his removal from power. Despite his best efforts, Khrushchev's attempts to modernize the Soviet state were ultimately his undoing.

Resistance and Opposition to Political Reforms

Throughout his rule, Nikita Khrushchev faced significant resistance and opposition to his political reforms, which ultimately played a crucial role in his downfall. This chapter explores the various factors that led to resistance and opposition, shedding light on the complex dynamics of power during the Cuban Missile Crisis and its aftermath.

Khrushchev's agricultural policies were a major point of contention within the Soviet Union. His attempts to modernize and increase agricultural production through collectivization and the Virgin Lands Campaign faced widespread resistance from farmers and local officials. The policies resulted in a decline in food production, leading to public discontent and an erosion of support for Khrushchev's leadership.

Another source of opposition came from the Soviet military, which was wary of Khrushchev's de-Stalinization campaign and his attempts to reduce its influence. The military's resistance to Khrushchev's policies was particularly evident during the Cuban Missile Crisis, where they openly challenged his decision to withdraw missiles from Cuba. Their opposition, coupled with Khrushchev's failure to consult them in advance, weakened his authority and contributed to his removal from power.

Economic reforms also played a significant role in Khrushchev's downfall. While his efforts to decentralize economic planning and increase consumer goods production were initially popular, they ultimately led to widespread inefficiencies and economic stagnation. This, combined with his inability to effectively address the country's economic challenges, further eroded support for his leadership.

Khrushchev's ambitious de-Stalinization campaign had a profound impact on his political standing. By denouncing Stalin's crimes and attempting to distance himself from his predecessor, Khrushchev alienated powerful factions within the Communist Party who still revered Stalin. This opposition, combined with his failure to adequately address the consequences of de-Stalinization, weakened his position and contributed to his downfall.

Khrushchev's handling of the Soviet space program also played a role in his fall from power. While his emphasis on space exploration initially garnered international acclaim, his failure to deliver on promised achievements and the costly failures of various space missions undermined his credibility and leadership.

Furthermore, Khrushchev's foreign policy decisions and his relationship with Eastern Bloc countries strained his leadership. His attempts to assert Soviet dominance and meddle in the affairs of these nations led to tensions and resistance, particularly from countries like China and Yugoslavia. These conflicts further weakened his position and contributed to his removal from power.

Lastly, Khrushchev's attempt to reform the Soviet political system was met with resistance from conservative forces within the party. His efforts to introduce a more collective leadership style and reduce the power of the Communist Party's Central Committee were seen as a threat to established hierarchies, resulting in opposition and ultimately his removal from power.

In conclusion, resistance and opposition to Khrushchev's political reforms, stemming from factors such as agricultural policies, the military, economic challenges, de-Stalinization, foreign policy decisions, and his attempt to reform the political system, all played a significant role in his downfall. Understanding these dynamics provides valuable insights into the intricate web of power and the complexities of leadership during the Cuban Missile Crisis and Khrushchev's rule.

The Impact of Political Reforms on Khrushchev's Rule

In the subchapter titled "The Impact of Political Reforms on Khrushchev's Rule," we delve into the various political reforms implemented by Nikita Khrushchev during his time in power and examine how they ultimately led to his downfall. This section of the book "The Cuban Missile Crisis: Unraveling Khrushchev's Rule" is addressed to a diverse audience consisting of diplomats, historians, and politicians, who are eager to gain a comprehensive understanding of the factors that contributed to Khrushchev's fall from power.

One of the significant aspects explored in this subchapter is the role of the Cuban Missile Crisis in the fall of Nikita Khrushchev. By analyzing the events leading up to the crisis and Khrushchev's handling of the situation, we shed light on how this highly tense and dangerous international standoff impacted his political standing and weakened his position within the Soviet Union.

Furthermore, Khrushchev's agricultural policies and their impact on his downfall are examined in detail. While his attempts to modernize and increase agricultural production were well-intentioned, they faced significant challenges and ultimately resulted in widespread dissatisfaction among the Soviet population. We explore the consequences of these policies and how they eroded Khrushchev's support base.

Another important aspect addressed in this subchapter is Khrushchev's relationship with the Soviet military and its role in his removal from power. By analyzing his handling of military matters and the conflicts that arose between him and the military leadership, we gain insights into the power struggles that ultimately contributed to his downfall.

Moreover, we analyze the role of economic reforms in Khrushchev's downfall. His attempts to shift the Soviet economy towards consumer goods production and de-emphasize heavy industry faced resistance and ultimately led to economic stagnation. By examining the consequences of these reforms, we gain a deeper understanding of their impact on Khrushchev's rule.

Additionally, Khrushchev's de-Stalinization campaign and its impact on his political standing are explored. This campaign, aimed at denouncing the excesses of Stalin's regime, sparked controversy and created divisions within the Soviet leadership. We examine the repercussions of this campaign and how it influenced Khrushchev's political standing.

Furthermore, we analyze Khrushchev's handling of the Soviet space program and its influence on his fall from power. By examining his ambitious space exploration initiatives and their consequences, we gain insights into how these decisions contributed to his downfall.

The subchapter also delves into Khrushchev's foreign policy decisions and their role in his downfall. By analyzing his approach towards the United States, Eastern Bloc countries, and other international actors, we explore how these decisions affected his political standing and ultimately led to his removal from power.

In addition, we examine Khrushchev's relationship with the Eastern Bloc countries and its impact on his removal from power. By analyzing the conflicts and tensions that arose between the Soviet Union and its satellite states, we gain insights into how these relationships played a role in Khrushchev's downfall.

Furthermore, we explore Khrushchev's attempt to reform the Soviet political system and its role in his downfall. By analyzing his efforts to introduce a more decentralized and participatory political structure, we gain insights into how these reforms were met with resistance and ultimately contributed to his removal from power.

Lastly, we delve into Khrushchev's personality and leadership style and how they contributed to his fall from power. By examining his impulsive behavior, propensity for making grandiose statements, and inability to effectively manage conflicts, we gain a deeper understanding of the personal factors that played a role in his downfall.

Overall, this subchapter provides a comprehensive analysis of the impact of political reforms on Khrushchev's rule. By examining a range of factors, from the Cuban Missile Crisis to his agricultural policies, relationship with the military, economic reforms, de-Stalinization campaign, space program, foreign policy decisions, Eastern Bloc relationships, political system reforms, and his personality and leadership style, we offer a multifaceted exploration of the factors that led to Khrushchev's fall from power.

The Overthrow of Khrushchev: Political Factors and Reforms

In the realm of Soviet history, the fall of Nikita Khrushchev is an event of significant importance. This subchapter delves into the multifaceted reasons behind Khrushchev's overthrow, exploring the political factors and reforms that ultimately led to his downfall. Addressing a diverse audience of diplomats, historians, and politicians, this analysis sheds light on the interplay between the Cuban Missile Crisis, Khrushchev's agricultural policies, his relationship with the Soviet military, economic reforms, de-Stalinization campaign, space program, foreign policy decisions, relationship with Eastern Bloc countries, attempt to reform the Soviet political system, and his personality and leadership style.

One of the key events that marked the decline of Khrushchev's rule was the Cuban Missile Crisis. This intense standoff between the United States and the Soviet Union highlighted Khrushchev's miscalculations and misjudgments, damaging his reputation both domestically and internationally. The consequences of this crisis reverberated throughout the Soviet political landscape, contributing to his eventual removal from power.

Furthermore, Khrushchev's agricultural policies played a pivotal role in his downfall. The Virgin Lands Campaign, aimed at boosting agricultural production, proved to be a failure, leading to food shortages and economic instability. The discontent among the Soviet population, coupled with the opposition from influential agricultural leaders, eroded Khrushchev's support and weakened his political standing.

The strained relationship between Khrushchev and the Soviet military also played a significant role in his removal from power. His attempts to reduce military spending and assert civilian control over the military hierarchy caused discontent among the military leadership. This discontent manifested in the form of a coup against Khrushchev, ultimately leading to his ousting.

Moreover, Khrushchev's economic reforms, aimed at modernizing the Soviet economy, faced considerable resistance from conservative elements within the party. His attempts to decentralize economic decision-making and introduce market-oriented policies encountered staunch opposition, further eroding Khrushchev's power and influence.

Khrushchev's de-Stalinization campaign, which aimed to distance the Soviet Union from the excesses of Stalin's era, had mixed results. While it initially garnered support, it also alienated influential party members and created a sense of instability within the party ranks. These factors ultimately contributed to Khrushchev's political standing being undermined.

Furthermore, Khrushchev's handling of the Soviet space program and his foreign policy decisions, including the Berlin Crisis and the U-2 incident, also played a role in his downfall. These events highlighted Khrushchev's impulsive decision-making and his inability to navigate complex international relations, further diminishing his standing both domestically and internationally.

Additionally, Khrushchev's strained relationship with the Eastern Bloc countries, particularly his mishandling of the Hungarian Revolution, weakened his support among socialist allies. This loss of support from the Eastern Bloc further isolated him within the Soviet political system.

Lastly, Khrushchev's attempt to reform the Soviet political system, including the introduction of collective leadership, faced resistance from within the party. His brash and unpredictable personality, coupled with his autocratic leadership style, alienated key party members and contributed to his eventual removal from power.

In conclusion, the downfall of Nikita Khrushchev was a complex interplay of political factors and reforms. The Cuban Missile Crisis, agricultural policies, relationship with the Soviet military, economic reforms, de-Stalinization campaign, handling of the space program and foreign policy decisions, relationship with Eastern Bloc countries, attempt to reform the political system, and his personality and leadership style all played a significant role in his removal from power. Understanding these dynamics provides valuable insights into the tumultuous era of Khrushchev's rule and its lasting impact on Soviet history.

Chapter 10: Khrushchev's Personality and Leadership Style and How They Contributed to His Fall from Power

Khrushchev's Personal Traits and Leadership Characteristics

Nikita Khrushchev, the leader of the Soviet Union during the Cuban Missile Crisis, was a complex figure with distinct personal traits and leadership characteristics that influenced his rule and ultimately contributed to his downfall. Understanding these aspects of his personality can provide valuable insights into the role he played in shaping the course of history.

Khrushchev's agricultural policies and their impact on his downfall are essential to examine. He implemented a series of agricultural reforms aimed at increasing productivity and reducing food shortages. However, these policies faced significant challenges and ultimately failed, leading to a decline in his popularity and eroding his political standing.

His relationship with the Soviet military was also a critical factor in his removal from power. Khrushchev's attempts to reduce the influence of the military and centralize power in the party created tensions within the ranks. This, combined with his mishandling of the Cuban Missile Crisis, strained his relationship with the military and weakened his grip on power.

Economic reforms also played a role in Khrushchev's downfall. His attempts to modernize the Soviet economy and shift resources from heavy industry to consumer goods faced resistance from the party bureaucracy. These reforms were seen as a threat to the established order, leading to opposition from within his own ranks and contributing to his eventual removal.

Khrushchev's de-Stalinization campaign, aimed at distancing the Soviet Union from the excesses of the Stalin era, had a profound impact on his political standing. While initially welcomed by the population, it alienated conservative elements within the party and ultimately weakened his position.

His handling of the Soviet space program and foreign policy decisions also played a role in his fall from power. Khrushchev's ambitions in space exploration and his aggressive foreign policy stance, particularly in relation to the United States, strained Soviet resources and resulted in costly failures. These setbacks further eroded his credibility and contributed to his removal.

Khrushchev's relationship with the Eastern Bloc countries and his attempts to reform the Soviet political system were also factors in his downfall. His attempts to assert Soviet dominance over the Eastern Bloc and implement political reforms faced resistance from the satellite states and conservative elements within the party, further destabilizing his rule.

Finally, Khrushchev's personality and leadership style were significant contributors to his fall from power. He was known for his impulsive and erratic behavior, often making decisions without consulting his advisors. This lack of consistency and his tendency to alienate allies and opponents alike undermined his credibility and weakened his position.

In conclusion, Khrushchev's personal traits and leadership characteristics, including his agricultural policies, relationship with the military, economic reforms, de-Stalinization campaign, foreign policy decisions, handling of the Soviet space program, and attempts to reform the political system, all contributed to his downfall. His impulsive and erratic personality and leadership style further exacerbated these challenges. By examining these aspects of his rule, we can gain a deeper understanding of the role he played in the Cuban Missile Crisis and the eventual unraveling of his leadership.

Public Perception and Reaction to Khrushchev's Personality

Nikita Khrushchev, the leader of the Soviet Union during the Cuban Missile Crisis, was a complex and controversial figure whose personality played a significant role in his eventual downfall. This subchapter delves into the public perception and reaction to Khrushchev's personality, shedding light on the various aspects that influenced his political standing.

Khrushchev's agricultural policies and their impact on his downfall were a key factor in shaping public perception. His ambitious plan to increase agricultural production through collectivization and the Virgin Lands Campaign faced numerous challenges and ultimately failed to yield the expected results. This failure led to widespread criticism and disillusionment among the Soviet population, eroding public faith in Khrushchev's leadership abilities.

Furthermore, Khrushchev's relationship with the Soviet military and its role in his removal from power also contributed to public perception. While Khrushchev initially enjoyed support from the military, his attempts to downsize and reorganize the armed forces were met with resistance. This strained relationship with the military affected public opinion, as many perceived Khrushchev as weak and indecisive in his handling of military matters.

Khrushchev's foreign policy decisions also played a significant role in shaping public perception and reaction. His aggressive stance during the Cuban Missile Crisis and his decision to place nuclear weapons in Cuba heightened tensions with the United States and the Western world. This brinkmanship strategy caused anxiety among the Soviet population and raised doubts about Khrushchev's ability to navigate international relations effectively.

Additionally, Khrushchev's personality and leadership style contributed to his fall from power. Known for his impulsive nature and erratic behavior, Khrushchev often made controversial public statements that created uncertainty both domestically and internationally. His de-Stalinization campaign, aimed at distancing the Soviet Union from the excesses of Stalin's rule, was met with mixed reactions. While some hailed it as a positive step towards reform, others viewed it as a betrayal of the Soviet ideology.

In conclusion, Khrushchev's personality and leadership style, along with his agricultural policies, foreign policy decisions, and relationship with the military, all played a role in shaping public perception and reaction to his rule. These factors ultimately contributed to his downfall as leader of the Soviet Union. By understanding the public's perception of Khrushchev and their reaction to his personality, historians, diplomats, and politicians can gain valuable insights into the fall of his rule and the broader implications of the Cuban Missile Crisis.

The Role of Khrushchev's Leadership Style in His Downfall

Throughout history, leaders' downfall can often be attributed to their leadership style and the decisions they make. Nikita Khrushchev, the Soviet leader during the Cuban Missile Crisis, was no exception. His unique leadership style played a significant role in his eventual removal from power.

One aspect of Khrushchev's leadership style that contributed to his downfall was his agricultural policies. Khrushchev introduced a series of reforms aimed at increasing agricultural productivity, such as the Virgin Lands Campaign. However, these policies proved to be ineffective and led to widespread food shortages and discontent among the Soviet population. This failure eroded his support and weakened his position within the Soviet government.

Furthermore, Khrushchev's relationship with the Soviet military also played a crucial role in his removal from power. He clashed with the military leadership over various issues, including the handling of the Cuban Missile Crisis. Khrushchev's decision to remove the missiles from Cuba without securing any concessions from the United States was seen as a sign of weakness by the military. This loss of prestige further undermined his authority and ultimately led to his removal.

Economic reforms were another factor that contributed to Khrushchev's downfall. While he introduced measures to modernize the Soviet economy, such as the Seven-Year Plan, these reforms were marred by inefficiency and mismanagement. The failure of these economic policies further eroded Khrushchev's credibility and support among the Soviet elite.

Khrushchev's de-Stalinization campaign also had a significant impact on his political standing. While initially popular, this campaign alienated many within the Soviet leadership who had been close associates of Stalin. The conservative faction within the Communist Party saw Khrushchev's denunciation of Stalin as a threat to their own positions of power, leading to a loss of support for Khrushchev and his eventual removal.

Additionally, Khrushchev's handling of the Soviet space program also influenced his fall from power. While he championed the Soviet Union's achievements in space, including the launch of Sputnik and the first manned spaceflight, his ambitious plans for lunar exploration were seen as unrealistic and costly. This, coupled with the failure of the Soviet lunar program, further damaged Khrushchev's reputation and weakened his position.

Khrushchev's foreign policy decisions and his relationship with Eastern Bloc countries also played a role in his downfall. His attempts to improve relations with the West, such as the negotiation of the Partial Nuclear

Test Ban Treaty, were unpopular among hardline Communist Party members who saw them as a betrayal of Soviet interests. Furthermore, Khrushchev's attempts to exert control over Eastern Bloc countries, particularly during the Hungarian Revolution of 1956, strained relations and led to increased opposition to his leadership.

Finally, Khrushchev's attempt to reform the Soviet political system also contributed to his downfall. His decision to decentralize power and give more autonomy to regional leaders weakened his own authority and created a power vacuum within the Soviet government. This, in turn, allowed his opponents to consolidate their power and ultimately remove him from office.

In conclusion, Khrushchev's downfall can be attributed to a combination of factors, including his agricultural policies, his relationship with the military, economic reforms, de-Stalinization campaign, handling of the space program, foreign policy decisions, attempts at political reform, and his leadership style. These factors, individually and collectively, eroded his support and weakened his position within the Soviet government, ultimately leading to his removal from power. Understanding the role of Khrushchev's leadership style is essential in unraveling the complex dynamics that shaped his rule and the events that unfolded during the Cuban Missile Crisis.

The Legacy of Khrushchev's Personality and Leadership Style

Nikita Khrushchev, the leader of the Soviet Union during the Cuban Missile Crisis, left behind a complex and controversial legacy. His personality and leadership style played a significant role in his rise to power, as well as his eventual downfall. This subchapter will explore the various aspects of Khrushchev's personality and leadership style and how they contributed to his fall from power.

Khrushchev's agricultural policies were a central component of his domestic agenda. His ambitious plan to increase agricultural production, known as the Virgin Lands Campaign, aimed to transform the Soviet Union into a superpower in both industry and agriculture. However, this policy ultimately led to disastrous consequences, including a decline in crop yields and widespread food shortages. The failure of his agricultural policies significantly undermined his political standing and contributed to his downfall.

Another crucial aspect of Khrushchev's leadership style was his relationship with the Soviet military. Despite his military background, Khrushchev often clashed with the military establishment. His attempts to assert civilian control over the military and implement reforms were met with resistance and opposition. These tensions with the military played a pivotal role in his removal from power, as the military leadership saw him as weak and indecisive.

Khrushchev's economic reforms, including the emphasis on consumer goods and the decentralization of economic decision-making, also had unintended consequences. While these reforms aimed to improve the living standards of the Soviet people, they led to inefficiencies and economic stagnation. The failure of these economic reforms undermined Khrushchev's credibility and contributed to his downfall.

Furthermore, Khrushchev's de-Stalinization campaign, which aimed to distance the Soviet Union from the brutal excesses of Stalin's regime, created significant political instability. This campaign sparked a backlash from conservative elements within the Soviet government and Communist Party, who opposed any revisionist policies. Khrushchev's attempts to reform the Soviet political system and his personality traits of impulsiveness and unpredictability further alienated him from his colleagues, leading to his eventual removal from power.

Khrushchev's foreign policy decisions also played a role in his downfall. The Cuban Missile Crisis, in particular, highlighted his reckless and confrontational approach to international relations. His decision to place nuclear missiles in Cuba without consulting his advisors or allies brought the world to the brink of nuclear war. This crisis further eroded his political standing and credibility, both domestically and internationally.

In addition to his foreign policy decisions, Khrushchev's relationship with the Eastern Bloc countries also contributed to his removal from power. His attempts to assert Soviet dominance over these countries and impose his own vision of socialism created resentment and resistance. The Eastern Bloc countries increasingly saw Khrushchev as a liability and a hindrance to their own interests.

Overall, Khrushchev's personality traits of impulsiveness, unpredictability, and confrontational approach to leadership, coupled with his flawed policies and decisions, ultimately led to his downfall. His agricultural policies, economic reforms, handling of the Soviet military, foreign policy decisions, and relationship with the Eastern Bloc countries all played a role in his removal from power. The legacy of Khrushchev's personality and leadership style serves as a cautionary tale, highlighting the importance of thoughtful and strategic decision-making in positions of power.